# Into the Dark

Born in Phoenix, Arizona, Allison DuBois became aware of her ability to communicate with departed souls when she was six. After a BA in Political Science from Arizona State University, she worked as an intern at the district attorney's office in Phoenix. This got her interested in using her skills to help solve crimes. Allison now devotes her life to helping the living by connecting them with deceased loved ones, and also by helping law enforcement agencies. She's the inspiration for the internationally popular TV series *Medium*, and a *New York Times* best-selling author.

Be sure to read her other books:

*Don't Kiss Them Good-Bye*

*We Are Their Heaven*

*Secrets of the Monarch*

*Talk to Me*

# Allison DuBois

# Into the Dark

## *Life through the eyes of the dead*

an Allison DuBois Book

*Published by Luck Maven Productions, LLC*

Lucky Maven Productions, LLC

Copyright © 2015 by Allison DuBois

designed by Joseph DuBois

All rights reserved, including the right to reproduce this book or portions thereof in any form whatsoever.

First edition October 2015

For order inquiries please contact :
Lucky Maven Productions sales
service@allisondubois.com or visit:
www.allisondubois.com

Manufactured in the United States of America
1 3 5 7 9 10 8 6 4 2
st

ISBN-13: 978-0-9761535-3-5
ISBN-10: 0-9761535-3-X

# Dedication

*I* would like to dedicate this book to my husband Joe and our daughters, Aurora, Fallon and Sophia. Without them I would lack the inspiration and the ability to write a book that's really about, love. A big thank you to the many people who share their stories here in an attempt to help those who walk their same path in grief. A special nod to the deceased who do their best to reach us and keep us moving forward.

# Contents

Introduction ix

| 1 | Dying | 1 |
| 2 | Mom and Dad | 32 |
| 3 | Pets are family | 57 |
| 4 | It's never too late | 66 |
| 5 | Communicating with the dead | 71 |
| 6 | Premature death | 107 |
| 7 | Dark endings | 132 |
| 8 | Bereavement | 167 |
| 9 | Relationships | 178 |
| 10 | Creating your version of heaven now | 194 |

# Introduction

I titled this book *Into the Dark* not referring to the deceased being in a dark place but rather the living who are in mourning, who are often surrounded by dark walls of depression. I want to go into the dark, to bring the living back to life, so that they can see the light again.

The deceased are living in sunshine and starlight, every moment that we miss them. They get to walk through all of the versions of heaven they had throughout their life, whether it be holding their baby for the first time, the first time they kissed the love of their life, their wedding day, a stroll in Paris, whatever filled their heart with joy.

The living grieve, we hide under the covers, we wish the

world away, we move through life filled with an empty hole that we can't seem to fill. The lucky ones are divinely sent someone to help them to see the light, but first those who care have to go into the dark, in order to understand where the grieving's heart and head is right now.

I'm writing this book for those of you who might be hard to reach, who died inside when you lost your loved one, those who need someone to throw you a lifeline. I'm going to show you life through the eyes of the dead, how they see our lives and how we still impact them. How they love us, root for us, and sit with us when we cry as we relive losing them. They're with us when we wake up and think for a moment that they're still alive, just to be destroyed again, as we remember the awful truth. They're with us every step of our journey as we struggle to find our way back to them.

It doesn't have to be over, you don't have to let go of them, you just need to learn how to hear them. I can teach you to do that, and I can help you to rejoin the living, so that you can create more happy days, days that after you die will be your versions of heaven.

# Dying

> Remember, when someone you love dies, there's a brief 'pause' before you get to be together forever. You only say goodbye once.
>
> – Allison DuBois

*A* soul is a gorgeous mystery that can't be dissected nor studied in a petrie dish, so right now, science can only hypothesize and speculate on theories concerning the survival of our souls. In their defense, at least scientists are trying to understand the essence of our spirit. Lately, it seems as though scientists and spiritualists are coming together, agreeing on more than we have in a very long time. But, for now, the proof of life-after-death lives in our hearts, because when the deceased are around us, our heart knows.

The dead are waiting for us to look for them and find them—not necessarily through a microscope, but rather through the memories in our hearts, in order to see them clearly. Souls are multifaceted, hypersensitive, polished versions of who they were in life. Their physical bodies couldn't contain their souls, and restricted them, now they can grow more loving, brighter and stronger than they were before.

The light of a soul from the Otherside could illuminate galaxies. Never worry about whether or not your deceased loved ones are okay; they become stronger every day as they grow closer to seeing you again. Souls become stronger because the living give them something to reach for, someone to live for. We are a version of their heaven, and they will one day become a part of our own heaven.

When I connect with a deceased person, I have to ask them how they felt at the time that they died in order to fully understand the level of trauma involved in the reading. We all can see how the living is affected by grief, but how are the deceased affected? We need to understand both sides, since the living and the dead will be eternally intertwined through the love that they share. The connection that the living and dead have can either cause pain, or bring joy to both, long after a person has physically died. I don't think that most people realize that the deceased continue to be affected by living people who they love, through the empathy that they feel for the grieving. When you hurt, they hurt. When you laugh, they laugh. They are emotional beings who choose to be our co-pilots throughout our lives. They can also continue to sample life through our experiences, so we make it possible for the deceased to travel, celebrate alongside of us, and see love through our eyes.

Once I've asked the deceased about their death, they begin to answer by allowing me to feel some of their pain, or lack of pain, sometimes even peaceful moments, that they experienced in their last minutes of life. Now, I know the process doesn't sound terribly pleasant but it is vital in a reading, it's crucial that I cross energy with the deceased, and what's more personal than them sharing their last breath, their very last thoughts, with me? Why do they share these with me? So that I can share them with you.

The sensations at the time of death vary; to me, a heart attack feels totally different than, say, an aneurysm. Carbon-monoxide poisoning feels nothing like getting hit by a car. There are more ways to die than people realize. By personally experiencing these variations of death, it helps me to understand how the deceased felt when they transitioned from life to the afterlife. I feel honored that the deceased choose to have such a personal moment with me; we're virtually strangers yet we're so vividly aware of one another's intentions. The deceased's motive for this bond with me is only so they can be heard by their living family and friends. It's necessary for them to align with my energy so that the messages to their loved ones resonate, and include important personal details of their lives for both parties to reflect upon. The deceased know that sometimes they only have one shot at getting their messages through to the people who matter to them the most, so they will give the process every bit of their energy in order to be heard. Their energy is fueled by the love that they took with them when they died, the love they still feel for us.

## What the dead see

No matter how someone dies, they usually see the same things, such as witnessing the person who finds their body or who is holding them in the moment that they passed. The sounds around them become clear and exaggerated, colors are more brilliant than when they were alive, they pop with vibrancy.

After they take in what's going on around their body, they will notice a person (or people), who steps forward in spirit, who is there to assure them that they're okay. It's almost always someone who previously died that the newly deceased ached to see, so their feelings become euphoric as they hug the one who had preceded them in death and waited for them for so long. If someone dies young and hasn't lost anyone close to them yet, then the deceased people who love the youth's parents come forward to comfort the child, along with other children who've died. Everyone that they loved and lost will wait for their embrace. Then introductions are made to the guardians who they never knew in life, but who have watched over them, and tried to keep them safe.

Since the deceased have no sense of time, the process of being received by the Otherside would seem lengthy to us, but in reality it happens fast enough that the newly departed has adapted and is able to witness the shockwaves that their death is sending through their family, friends and community. They can see their parents getting the phone call that they had dreaded since the very day their child was born. Others can see their spouse being notified, their children being woken up by the commotion in their house, the news that has been received detailing their death; they see it all.

The departed always attend their memorials and funerals, they hang on to every word spoken about them, they wipe tears from the faces of those they love, and their need to communicate is born!

The music that you carefully select for their funeral, the clothes that you pick out for them, the pictures that you share, along with the memories that you have, it all matters monumentally to them. They take note of who is at their memorial, and even who chose not to come—yep, they are very aware. They don't hold grudges, but they do recognize who needed to show up for them. They're usually surprised at how many acquaintances, even strangers, come out of respect.

Men who pass tend to prefer money/energy to be spent on food and drink for their wake, rather than flowers. Think of the person whose life you're memorializing, and try to honor them with their unique personality in mind. The deceased love seeing the small details of their life celebrated and enjoyed by their loved ones. They'd rather listen to the 'toasts' in their honor more than just about anything, because it's one of the few occasions during their wake where they can feel the broken hearts of their loved ones lighten just a little, and it's then that they know that everything's going to be okay. The people they love will laugh, love and find happiness throughout their lives, and when they die they can tell them all about it.

The deceased reflect on their life, and they see how they affected the people around them. This is the instant that some spirits realize that they have a regret they can't change as easily as they could have when they were alive. The need to communicate with the living continues to build with their regret or with their need to soothe the living. In my experience, the deceased will try their hand at communicating immediately, and if they can't reach the person they want to, then they will go through a friend, or a friend of a friend, anyone who will listen and, sometimes, that person ends up being me.

## THE GRASS IS GREENER?

Whether or not you die suddenly or slowly, there are various debatable pro's and con's. When you die over an extended period from, say, a disease, you have time to say your goodbyes and get your affairs in order. On the other hand, the living has to see you suffer, and you must endure the pain and all the feelings that go along with the process of dying. When a person dies in an accident, or suddenly, , it leaves many stunned and with a feeling of no closure, no getting to say goodbye. The only upside is the deceased's pain wasn't drawn out over weeks, months or even years.

When people grieve yet innately know their loved ones are thriving in spirit, the deceased feel both relieved and proud. They don't have to work as hard to get through to us, and the communication is more upbeat and instantaneous.

On the other hand, grieving people who feel dead inside, who feel they also died the day they lost their loved one, they're more work for the deceased to connect with spiritually. This kind of pain almost feels like a black hole, that grows and eats up the grieving person's soul; they literally die inside. This is one of many reasons why I work so hard to teach the living how to connect with the deceased, it's a way to help the living to let go of the kind of grief that erodes their soul, much like a cancer would.

Once the pain is brought down to a level that the deceased can get past, the communication can be felt by the grieving. When the communication is felt by the grieving, then the healing begins, the signs will start coming frequently, and slowly the grieving person begins to feel, and see, their deceased loved one all around them. This is when the deceased know that they've achieved reconnection, and their relationship with the living is still intact.

When someone dies young or quickly, they are less likely to want to leave the living, so they usually choose to remain around their living family. They aren't bound here in limbo, they stay because they want to, and they move between the living and the dead freely.

Children who die often have their room kept as a shrine to them, but let's try not to think of this as morbid or unhealthy. The parents often get the urge to keep the child's room the same in order to feel closer to their child, but also the urge comes from the deceased child telling their parents that they are still a part of the family, and they aren't ready to leave. This demonstrates communication between the parents and their child, and it's a coping mechanism on both sides, so I see it as healthy for some, until both parties are truly ready to move forward together, in a brand new relationship, a spiritual one. However, the deceased child sees their room the way it was when they died, whether the furniture is there anymore or not, so the shrine tends to be more for the living. In my experience, parents tend to be ready to begin to move forward after a few years and even remodel their child's room, and that's a good thing for them. In a deceased child's world, their room will always look the way they remember it, they don't feel forgotten when we change it, because to them it will always look just how they liked it. Deceased children want to be a part of their parents' lives still, they like to be talked about at the dinner table, and they love watching home movies!

People who die when they're elderly tend to transition effortlessly because they've lived a full life and often they're even eager to see all of the people they've lost over the years. The elderly revert to the age that they were the happiest in life, and unless they have a living spouse that they believe still needs them, they will spend more time catching up with their deceased friends and relatives, popping in occasionally to look in on their children and grandchildren.

The memories that you're making right now will one day become your versions of heaven to be replayed over and over again, so make sure you have lots of incredible memories to satisfy you in the afterlife. I always tell people to '*live life large*'. You can either spend your whole life wading in the kiddie pool where it's safe, or you can climb the tall ladder and jump off the diving board into the deep end of life to feel the exhilaration of taking a chance. I personally enjoy the high-dive.

## What do the dead do every day?

The deceased constantly come through reminding me that,

'The dead are more alive than the living,' because they don't carry the emotional baggage that we (the living) often do.

The deceased aren't fear-based like the living tend to be, they want to experience anything new to them through us, because their life has ended and without us they don't continue to create memories, so in a way we're their chance for new experiences. They can relive the happiest days of their lives over and over again, but they need their emotional tie to us in order to travel and enjoy something new. Technically, they can go to those places without us, but it doesn't mean anything to them if we're not there, too.

I was on a television talk show and a woman who had lost her husband asked me, "What does he do every day?"

Her husband described a bar with pool tables, and he said he really liked to be there.

She replied, "Oh, that's where we met!"

I told her, "Well, every day he gets to meet you for the first time again."

I thought that was one of the most romantic things that I'd ever witnessed, a reminder that true love has no end.

When I bring through the deceased, they revert to a part of their life when they were the happiest, and they repeat the days that brought them joy. In a way, it's what they want for us, they want us to build on the happy experiences in our lives, and not take those valuable moments for granted. As our years start to feel like mere days, and we rush forward in life, they'd like nothing more than for us to recognize how splendid the people around us are, so that we can tell them now, when it matters the most.

Children who pass over relive their childhoods and immerse themselves in their family and friends. They talk about their dad carrying them on his shoulders, and their mom holding their hand, brushing their hair or making them a sandwich; these are everyday occurrences that we often don't think sticks with our children. I'm here to tell you that it does stay with them, they forever carry those moments like butterflies in their hearts, and when they die they take all of those moments with them.

Spouses who pass over relive their wedding day or the birthdays of their children. They talk about still being there for their wedding anniversary with their living spouse. As we physically age, the deceased spouses still see us as younger, so as they sit beside you holding your hand, they see you through smitten eyes. An 80-year-old will appear to the deceased to be the age they were when they fell in love, and that will never change. They will never see you age, because they look at you through their heart.

The deceased prod us to travel, live life zealously, and revel in the small joys that surround us on a daily basis. When we create new memories, even though the deceased aren't here physically, make no mistake they are still here. In my readings the deceased encourage my clients to go to the place where they first met, or where they spent their summer vacations together, knowing they're going to have company. Even though you can't always see them when you'd like to, that doesn't mean they're not there. The deceased tell me that when *we* die, they will show us, much like a movie, the holidays and special moments that occurred in our lives *after* their physical death. In these replays of our lives, we get to see where they were, where they stood beside us, when they laughed with us. Sometimes they held our hand—you'll be able to see that happen—sometimes they kissed us on the cheek, or stroked our hair—you'll be able to witness this through their eyes. It's extraordinary to think of, and to know that, we'll one day experience this alongside of them, it is an incredibly beautiful thought.

So, you see, along with them having the option to be with their deceased loved ones, or relive some of their brightest memories from their lives with us, they also have the option to participate in our daily lives. Days they will replay for us when we cross over, so that we can see how we continued to bring them life, long after they died!

## RECONNECTING IN READINGS: REMINISCING WITH THE DEAD

I thought it would be helpful to give you some examples of the sort of information that comes through in readings. It's one thing for me to explain how it works when spirits are brought through, it's entirely another to absorb the personal details that the deceased are compelled to share with their loved ones in readings. The details when connected give us a vibe of the personality and a visual of the physical characteristics of the deceased. The messages are intended to improve our lives, but that can't happen until the deceased break down the emotional walls of the living, reaching them by touching their soul through the familiarity of their presence validated through specific details in the reading.

The deceased orchestrate a reading to take place when the

time is right, I've seen it too many times to question their motives. A reading quite often gets booked or moved (if I get sick) and just happens to fall on the anniversary of the birth or death of the deceased, or some significant date shared between the living and the departed. There are so many variables to a reading that I believe the best way for you to understand what a reading feels like is for you to look at some moving personal stories for yourself.

## Gina's story: Finding Dad

I should begin by saying that the Universe and in particular, my dad, brought me into contact with Allison four times in a two-year period, until I had my reading and was able to get the messages I needed to hear.

My husband and I attended a book-signing, and we had an opportunity to have Allison sign three of her books, and we met Joe there, too. They were both charming and we asked Allison at the signing table about our furry wonder who had passed on eight months earlier. Allison took the time to ease our grief and let us know that our beloved pets, the furry, feathered and scaled, are in heaven with our loved ones who have passed over and that we will see them again. She laughed and mentioned that her daughters' many pets were waiting for them on the other side with a very exasperated caretaker wondering how many pets the girls would be getting over their lifetime. This was wonderful to hear, and for those of us who have a bond with our 'pets' that is more like that of parent–child, it is a joy to know.

After meeting Allison at the book-signing, I went to her

website and found a listing for what I later learned is an annual event Allison holds around Mother's Day in Phoenix. It is a group appearance with a chance to see how Allison works when she is bringing people through. I bought tickets and my husband and I attended the Mother's Day event in 2012. It was a very moving experience and Allison brought through loved ones for people who had lost children and parents, brothers, husbands and wives. I held my husband's hand and thought about how lucky I was as I heard people confirming what Allison was experiencing as she brought through their loved ones.

Here is where I need to explain a bit about my circumstances. I have always been what they used to call 'high-strung' and what in New York we call 'neurotic'. But after I lost my dad in 1999, I began a steady decline into depression, anxiety and, after a series of disabling eye surgeries in 2005, eventual agoraphobia and a total withdrawal from the world and living.

The natural progression today by many medical professionals treating someone presenting with my condition is through a series of medications—antidepressant, anti-anxiety and, for some, antipsychotic—and therapy, and/or eventual hospitalization. Often this is done in tandem with the prescribing of painkillers and sedatives to 'mask' the physical and/or spiritual pain the patient is experiencing.

Here, let me say this is in no way a rejection of the relief that many people experience through medication, and this is not a Tom Cruise jumping on the couch moment, either.

This is an anecdotal recounting of one woman's experience, and no one should 'go off their meds', as they say, without a helluva safety net of family, friends and medical professionals, and if you find any parallels with my experience, perhaps it will help you to move through your grief, as I have learned to.

So, since 2007, I can count on two hands the times that I left my house for anything other than groceries, or doctor visits, and then I did it at the crack of dawn, or close of business, in order to avoid people. The best way that I can describe the anxiety I was feeling is to take the nervous butterflies of your first time on stage, or your wedding day, and multiply it times a million. The butterflies become a gnawing, gaping hole of fear, that is almost constantly with you. The medications attempt to fill the hole. In my case, the medications would often fil the hole I carried around in my sternum, but after 60 to 90 days on the medications the feeling would come back. By the time I attended Allison's book-signing in 2012, I was on a fairly high dose of anti-anxiety and antipsychotic medications, and I was not feeling up to leaving the house. To say I had stopped living would not be an exaggeration.

But I was positively, urgently drawn to the events where Allison was appearing. To my great surprise, Joe emailed in July 2012 with an opening for a personal reading. Here is where I threw a spanner in the works, so to speak—a reading became available the day before my dad's birthday, August 3, 2012. If you have read Allison's earlier books, or heard her speak about her work, you know that spirits like to play with calendar dates to give us messages, to assure us that it's them. I felt my dad wanting to talk to me, but I knew my husband, love of my life, had all his loved ones on the other side. So I scheduled a reading for him with Allison, instead of for me.

My husband's experience was exactly what he needed. When

he came home, he told me he felt like he had twenty years of therapy and I must, must have a reading. On June 23, 2013, I did just that and I haven't been the same since.

Going in to meet with Allison, I had several moments of sheer panic wondering exactly what in the hell I was doing. Since a huge part of my neurosis involved me being down on myself, I slid easily into 'What if Allison looks into my soul and it is like the Portrait of Dorian Gray—hideous?!' These doubts were nothing in comparison to the feeling of total absolute certainty that I was supposed to have this reading.

The night before the reading, I sat in my living room with my husband and I wrote out my questions for my dad, who I hoped would come through, and the top five questions that consume me and spin up my anxiety, day in and day out.

I had my notepad in my purse as Allison began, asking me if there was someone in particular I wanted to bring through. I told her I was hoping to speak to my dad, and she asked if I had more than one father on the Otherside. And, actually, I do. I let Allison know I was also hoping to speak to my stepdad, the man who raised me.

Allison went quiet for a minute or two, drawing on her pad, and then she brought my dad through for me. He connected right away, and Allison said he was coming through 'fast 'n furious'. Then he started answering every question that I had written the night before on the notepad which was in my purse, without me asking them.

I told him how sorry I was for not appreciating him when I was younger, and for all the grief I gave him as a teenager. My dad died at 54, and at age 31 I had only begun to appreciate him, and what an incredible man he was. I cannot describe the feeling from hearing my dad's reply. Allison said he was shaking his head, and telling her, 'All kids are like that with their parents, and it's the cycle of life. No kids appreciate their parents when they're young.'

Allison said I was right, he did 'belong to me', that I brought meaning to his life when I came into it. That he needed to be needed. Allison told me he was laboring her breathing, and she felt heaviness in her chest. I let her know he died from congestive heart failure and had been suffering from Chronic Obstructive Pulmonary Disease before he died.

Allison said something really important to me then: "He says you may feel heaviness in your chest since he died." When Allison spoke those words, I felt something shift in my chest. I think in Japanese Buddhism they call it a moment of satori, when you feel suddenly enlightened.

Then my dad went on to answer every other question on my list. He told Allison he is with the boy. And he said I did a 'good job with the boy'. That is my son who was born a year after my father died. On the notepad I had written, 'I know my dad is watching over Megan (my daughter) but is anyone with the boy?' I had written 'the boy' and that is how he answered.

Then Allison said, "He has the dogs." That was the third question on the notepad, still sitting in my purse.

Allison told me my dad was showing her my wedding. At the time I thought he might be expressing regret for not being able to attend my wedding, but something else Allison said gave me an additional insight later. She said my dad could put pictures in my head. Later in the reading she was suggesting I sit on a bench by a fountain with a hummingbird feeder to relax in my yard. I let her know I have a fountain and a family of hummingbirds in the yard, and I had been picturing a bench to put under the tree since my dog had passed. That's my dad putting the picture in my head, communicating with me through the pictures, so I can sit with him, and my dogs, on that bench.

For the past year, I have been telling my husband and kids that I wish we could renew our wedding vows for our twentieth anniversary this year. I have been picturing us outside, in Pinetop, Arizona, renewing our vows. While he is showing Allison my wedding, my dad's telling me he will be there to walk me down the aisle.

Then my dad started answering the questions I had written out to ask Allison when we got to the 'Life Reading' portion of the reading. Allison said he was showing her a For Sale sign. My first life-reading question was about the health and safety of the kids, and the next was whether I should sell my house. I told Allison I had planned to ask her about moving, and so she took a look to see what's coming my way down the pike.

Allison said she sees me in Scottsdale, and Pinetop, which is exactly where I want to be. I laughed when Allison said she could see me happy on my porch up in Pinetop full-time after the kids are grown.

She said my house would sell if I wanted, and we are now working on exactly that. I could never have conceived of selling the house; it was a shelter against what I perceived as a cruel world before my reading.

My dad gave me a few messages for my mother during the reading. I sighed deeply when he started talking about how much he loves my mother; I share the 'Marcia, Marcia, Marcia, it's always about Marcia' syndrome that Jan Brady had in that regard. But the words he had for my mother were important, and I shared his messages with her when I called her later in New York.

My dad achieved another miracle of sorts with that, because since that call, my mother and I have been speaking several times a week, and we have been appreciating each other, something that we struggled with in the past.

This is the most important effect from the reading, though—the day I met with Allison was the last day that I took any medication for anxiety or depression. A week later, I stopped taking pain medication as well.

Now the reason this is an incredible thing, and not just nice, is that due to the length of time I have been on these types of medications, the physicians don't take people off them after that length of time. I have tried to get off them a few times, most recently last Christmas, and after a day, the feeling of anxiety in my chest would cripple me, and I would wind up on Xanax to get me back down.

One of the tools that Allison gave me was to visualize. I picture my dad every night, at the foot of my bed, holding a basket. Then I ask him to take the things from me I cannot handle. In my case, I ask him to take my anxiety, my depression, my physical and emotional pain, and any withdrawal I may feel. Now, after three years on three painkillers daily, I should have had some extreme discomfort for a short period. That didn't happen. I waited every day to feel sick, anxious and terrified, but it never happened.

## DYING

I have not had an anxiety attack since I had my reading with Allison, and my dad took away the self-imposed burden that I was living under.

Allison told me my dad wanted me to *LIVE*. And for the first time in six years I want to live, too.

Two weeks after I met with Allison, I went and met with my congressman at his office to give him feedback on some current events. I went by myself in a cab. I sat on a bench outside the office in a small urban park in North Scottsdale in a commercial area waiting for my appointment. I had my iPod on and I was listening to music, and I was looking at the big puffy clouds and not feeling anxious at all. (Previously, sitting alone outside would be cause for cascading panic attacks.) I was looking up at the sky and asking my dad to give me a sign in the clouds. Just then, a huge brown eagle started circling above my head. Now, I have been in Arizona for twenty years but I'm still a New York City girl at heart, and I was like, 'Wow! Look at that giant bird swooping around!' And it kept circling me, five times, six, seven. So then I started looking for prey that the eagle might be circling, but it just kept circling above this tiny office park on the highway, and I was the only person outside, just sitting on a little bench. So finally I thought, 'Hey, let me take a picture!' And I started snapping pictures with my iPod. The enormous bird stayed above me for almost ten minutes, and I got a few great pictures before it left.

Allison says spirit will send you a sign, often a bird if the deceased felt trapped in their broken body in some way before they died, and they want to demonstrate to you their freedom of spirit. I asked my dad for a sign in the sky and I got one!

## Into the Dark

The universe had been sending me signs since the reading. The Friday before I met with the congressman I received an automated email from the local library system notifying me of an entry-level job opening. I had filled out the 'interest card' years earlier. I went ahead and applied.

To make it even more improbable, I was so forward as to ask my congressman for a personal reference for that job application since I haven't worked in so long, and after an hour of lively debate on a host of issues, he said he was happy to give me a reference.

About three weeks after the reading, as I felt more myself than I had in a decade, I got my 'travel' bug back. I wanted to go to Italy. I wanted to go on a Perillo Tour like the commercials I grew up seeing in New York City. I made a jar with pics of Florence, Rome and Venice, and I throw money in there every chance I get.

The day after I made the Italy jar, I received Allison's monthly newsletter, which you can sign up for on her website. In it she quoted a passage from the book she was working on, in which she explains that spirit wants us to *TRAVEL*. That they are with us at these events in our lives. I laughed as it felt like the universe was validating me again. I put up some photos of a trip I took many years ago to visualize travel in the future. There is a spot next to my mom in one group photo, that my eye is drawn to whenever I pass it now. It is an empty spot, but I don't think it's really empty. My dad is there with us, and when I pass on he will show me that he was standing right there, where I knew he was.

An important tool Allison gave me was simple but incredibly important for me. Allison acknowledged that my personality type is one in which I try to force my will upon the universe and 'make' things happen. Often I am trying to force my agenda on the pattern of the universe, and all I get is grief in return. Allison says when she feels a stubborn desire to force something to happen, she does a simple breathing exercise: 'Breathe in willingness, breathe out willfulness.' I now make it a point to do this a few times a day.

I don't know how long I've been fighting the universe, but I used to feel exhausted and stressed every minute of every day. Now I feel energized and free, like I'm living a series of gifts from the universe, and I can't wait to see what happens next. I'm not afraid anymore.

So, really, Allison gave me back my life when she brought my dad through. I don't know how many people have anxiety due to a chemical imbalance, or how many are spiritually wounded the way I was, be it self-inflicted needless guilt, or trauma, experienced on this side of the veil. Now I know that with Allison's help and my dad's guidance, I am able to trust the universe and just let go. Let go of the guilt, let go of the all-consuming worry, the frenzy of nerves, and the endless what if's? The constant self-loathing for every mistake and every sin. It is gone. It is quiet in my sternum, the butterflies are free.

## THE DECEASED'S PERSPECTIVE

Gina was experiencing a sort of *soul paralysis* trying to move through the grief after losing her dad. The anxiety and pain that she felt caused her life to be thrown into a tailspin.

Gina's dad was able to intervene from the Otherside, and

reach her through me; he literally brought her to me so that she could find her way out of the fog that she'd been in due to her despair. I don't think that most people realize how thin the veil is between the living and the deceased, it's like a fragile, silk curtain.

From Gina's dad's perspective, he had to sit back and watch his daughter suffer, he had to listen to her talk to him and cry. Imagine the energy that welled inside of him, until he had enough energy built up to help change the course of Gina's life. Her dad was able to breathe life back into his daughter and surround her with his energy comprised from love.

The deceased can make things happen in the physical world by focusing their emotion on us, and willing it to happen. The book-signing with the public speech where I originally met Gina was only done by me as a favor for an old high-school friend. I really wasn't there for any other reason, or so I thought. Maybe Gina's dad orchestrated me being at that event. We never really know in life why we're placed in people's lives. Sometimes, unbeknown to us, we're moved there by the powers that be, the souls who are acting to save someone they love. Gina's dad seemed to be doing just that. As a dad, he was probably protecting his daughter, just as he would have done in life. The kicker is that we're stronger when we die, the emotional power that spirits possess is nothing that we can fully fathom, it's a powerful love that can transform darkness into light and pain into joy.

Gina's an example of someone whose dad had lived a full life; he grew up, he had a family, and his family and friends, even though they miss him terribly, understand that it's the natural order for a parent to die first. The next story is Kristy's and it's the polar opposite of Gina's loss—it's about a mother who outlived her children. The loss that most people fear the most is *'loss of children'*. It's not the natural order for children to proceed us in death, but it happens more often than any of us want to admit. The unimaginable pain involved in losing a child can't be compared to any other loss in the world, it's the Mount Everest of grief.

## LIVING AGAIN

I felt like doing something for my Facebook friends, so I decided to give two VIP tickets to any of my scheduled events to the person whose story received the most 'likes'. I thought I'd leave it up to the people on my site to do something for someone who really needed it. After a week of voting, a winner emerged, a woman whose husband had died tragically while she was pregnant. I was genuinely touched by all the stories that people shared with me, and I think my Facebook Friends enjoyed being involved.

But afterwards something still bothered me about the person who had received the second-most votes, a woman who had lost three of her four children, one as recent as a couple of months prior to my ticket giveaway. I had a lump in my throat for a couple of weeks and it was as if someone was pushing me to reach out to her. My head hurt, and her story whirled around in my mind, as if to say to me, 'I'm not going away'. So I reached out to her and offered to read her pro bono, in order to ease both our minds on some level. Kristy is her name, and she was all-in, so she drove from Seattle, Washington, to Scottsdale, Arizona, for our reading.

When Kristy walked in, she felt to me as if she hadn't taken a breath in a very long time, as if her heart had stopped beating, but her body had physically continued without it. She had brought along her mother for moral support, which I thought was wise. That day, I wasn't feeling so good myself, I had a cold, but it was now or never so I began preparing for the reading by moving my pencil across my notepad in my usual way and immediately Kristy's children came through.

We started with her son, Anthony. I wrote the number 16 and asked Kristy if Anthony made it to the age of sixteen; she replied that's how old he was when he died. He talked about his mobile phone being important, and Kristy said she felt guilty for not making him take it with him on that day. One of the first things Anthony said to tell his mom was, 'Not to feel guilty, she didn't do anything wrong.' He was trying to ease the pain that she carried for not making him take his phone; his message was well received.

Anthony kept pointing to my chest area, the place where a necklace would rest. I asked Kristy if she wore a necklace for her kids, and she reached into her T-shirt and pulled out a hidden necklace with bangles on it commemorating her children. He talked about a trip to California and Disneyland being his version of heaven. Kristy then explained that before her daughter Kristina had died, they all went as a family to Disneyland, and they had the time of their lives, one of their last, best days together. I told her to put up the pictures taken at Disneyland, so that she could see how happy she made her kids.

Like a usual sixteen-year-old, Anthony talked about sports, his football team, and said he loved his sports memorabilia. In particular, he said he'd collected many souvenirs of his 'favorite team'—a reference that Kristy understood exactly. His remains were in a Seattle Seahawks urn, his favorite team! Anthony shared many other touching messages with his mother and grandmother, and then it was time for us to turn to Kristina.

Kristy's daughter came through with a completely different energy than her brother had exhibited. She talked about having a wild streak, and not always listening to her mother, but she wanted Kristy to know how much she had always loved her. Kristina talked about feeling nauseous and vomiting at the time of her death, which was confirmed by her mother. She wanted her mom to know that she was feeling content now, and not unwell at all.

Kristina also wanted to let her family know that she was around—from such things as making the dogs bark, to seeing her photos displayed proudly everywhere, as well as the message on her headstone. The information stirred many emotions in her mother, but I could see some of Kristy's pain leave her and her breathing became more relaxed.

Anthony and Kristina are peacefully together, though they still razz each other like most brothers and sisters do. They are also with Kristy's baby Kynslei, their deceased sister, who the older siblings watch over. Kynslei, died when she was quite young, so she didn't have a lot to communicate to me. Yet, she remains a part of the tapestry of her mother's life both past and present. The children choose to still exist along side of their mother as they help guide her on her life's journey. The spiritual trio can move back and forth between the spirit world and the physical one, being active with their deceased loved ones, as well as their living family.

At the end of Kristy's reading, Anthony took credit for bringing us together. His grandmother then shared with me an amazing fact: After missing out on the free tickets in my Facebook contest, Kristy's mom took a day off work to pray to Anthony that he would get me to contact her. Twenty-four hours later, I contacted Kristy about a reading. Good job, Anthony!

### Kristy's story: Answered Prayer

First off, I want to say that I have prayed for a reading from Allison for a long time, but this time I begged for it!

The first thing that I noticed right after receiving Allison's Facebook message to arrange my reading was that we both lived on a street with the same name, but more than 2000 miles apart.

The second thing that happened was that I had brought along my copies of Allison's three books, which I had purchased over the years, so I could ask her to sign them, but I was so excited and nervous I left them in the car. When I walked in to meet her, she had a book in her hands, already signed and ready to give me. The funny thing is, that book was the only one of Allison's that I didn't already have, and she didn't know this, so now I have the complete set.

As we sat down and Allison prepared to start my reading, she asked which child I wanted to communicate with first. She then explained that it was like my children were fighting over which one of them was my favorite and who was going first—something all of my kids often did was fight over who was supposedly my favorite As hard as it was to choose, I wanted to speak first with my only son, Anthony, whose death was most recent and fresh in my mind. The death that was truly killing me all over again inside.

Allison said that her head hurt, and that she could not breathe in her chest area. Anthony had been in a bad car accident that ejected him from the vehicle before it landed on him. This, to me, was why Allison was feeling that he couldn't breathe in his chest area, and his cause of death was due to the severe head trauma from being thrown from the vehicle.

First thing Anthony wanted me to know was that I was the 'best mom ever'. And he said there is nothing I could have done to change the outcome.

Anthony brought up his mobile phone, and this was so significant to me because of the guilt I had about this. I usually did not let him go anywhere without a direct line of communication between us. He was my 'baby' and I had already buried two other children before him. I thought I was a terrified and paranoid mother due to all the deaths that I had to deal with in my life. Anthony had broken his phone, and he didn't tell me until the last minute. I really didn't want to let him go until the new phone arrived in the mail. For some reason, the delivery took longer than usual and arrived two days after his death.

Anthony also mentioned all the balloons and thanked me for them. These were the many balloons we had written messages on and released at his memorial service. They were his favorite color, too.

In the reading, Anthony said he loved movies, pizza, etc.—all true—but he talked most about his beloved NFL and football games, which was typical of him! Then he spoke about his sports memorabilia and his 'favorite team' and I knew he was referring to the urn: I had just ordered his urn, and I had chosen a design featuring his favorite special team, the Seattle Seahawks, in their blue color with their emblem on it. Allison said he loved it. I had also gone to the homecoming game for Stanwood, Anthony's old team, as I thought that was something he would have wanted us to do. We used to love going to football games together and with friends. Even though it was too hard for me to stay for the whole game, I went and tried to make an effort for Anthony. Now it was reassuring to know that he'd been there with me.

Anthony also said that he was happy with what I was doing with his room and keeping it the same because he likes to hang out in there. I had told all of my family and friends that I am not changing his room and it will remain the same forever! He talked about a picture of us holding each other—there is one like this in his bathroom—and how he has his arms around me.

Allison said Anthony was with me all of the time, and saw that I was not buying groceries, making meals at home or eating well anymore. This was true, and had been since the day he passed. I just didn't care anymore or even have it in me to do anything anymore. He said he wanted me to cook a turkey for Thanksgiving and to buy a gift for a child for him at Christmas. I had already spoke to someone in private earlier that month about the idea of Christmas gifts in honor of each of my children. I had thought that Anthony and Kristina both would love that.

*Dying*

He wasn't, however, as keen on the tattoo idea and he made this clear! He knew that many of us, family and friends, are thinking about getting a tattoo for him or in his honor, and while he was a little amused by that, he wanted each of us to really think about it and make sure we got something we wanted. The funny thing is, I'd often wanted to stop at my favorite tattoo place in Tucson, Arizona but was always pressed for time and not quite sure about what to get done, so I had decided to wait and think about it a little longer.

Anthony said he knew he had made some bad choices. He revealed that he'd thought he was going to die young, but not that young. He was also worried about some of his friends who survived and about them having survivor's guilt and not wanting to live anymore.

The necklace that Anthony brought up has great meaning and significance to me. The way I wear it, you do not see it on me most of the time so people don't know it's there. It is the same necklace that my daughter was wearing when she died five years earlier in Tucson. I never wore a necklace before, but now I have never taken it off. Anthony knew what it meant to me.

Allison described Anthony as another James Dean and said that he was a ladies man—boy, was he ever! My son had girls chasing him when he was still in diapers! It was crazy at times. She said that Anthony has chosen to stay at the age of sixteen in his version of heaven. Apparently, he is also there to help his sister Kristina with her emotional issues around her passing. My daughter Kristina was battling depression when she died and she told Allison that, 'She was nauseous and sick to her stomach when she passed away,' which was true. She also said that before she died it had seemed as if nothing would help her depression, and how this affected her.

Kristina said that she shows herself in the form of music a lot and that she sees her pictures everywhere. She also has all of our dogs that have passed and is taking care of them.

After Anthony passed away, my four-year-old bulldog became sick, which I thought was due to stress; the dog had died on the Tuesday before we met on the weekend with Allison, who didn't know about this. Also, at the time of Anthony's death, we had a litter of puppies that were a month old and one of those had got sick and died as well.

Kristina also said she is with my current dogs, too. She has always loved animals of all kinds but especially our dogs that we had throughout her life. She told us something that amazed me: When Anthony passed away I decided to keep one of the puppies and named him 'Little Ace' in honor of my son. Recently, Little Ace has been going to Anthony's old bathroom, where he stands at the door tilting and turning his head while barking at what seems to be nothing. I thought it was Anthony messing with me because I use to kid him about all the time he spent in the bathroom. Kristina let me know that it isn't Anthony, it's her playing with the puppy.

My daughter also did not want to talk of her passing, as she, too, knew that she had made some bad choices, which led to her death at the age of eighteen. However, Allison said that Kristina chose to remain at the age of nine, as that was her happiest time in her life. This is about how old she was when her dad and I tried to reconcile one more time. Allison also mentioned that Kristina said she was a 'Daddy's girl'. Little did Allison know that

Kristina's headstone has the words 'Daddy's girl' in the centre of it. Kristina really did adore her father, and during the reading she asked about him and said she will be waiting for him and will catch him when he falls. Unfortunately, less than a year later Kristina's dad died, one year to the day that Anthony had passed away, I'm sure that's what she meant by 'catching him'. Kristina and her dad are together again.

I now know that Kristina and Anthony will not physically return in my lifetime, but my children and my other loved ones will be waiting for me when I cross over and that gives me a sense of peace. Until then, they are all the time watching over me, being here with me always.

## THE DECEASED'S PERSPECTIVE

When I read for Kristy, I brought a son and daughter through for their mother and it was very emotional, it felt like being a 'spiritual surgeon'. You have to open up the person's heart with the words from the deceased, in order to allow the pain in their heart to begin to release. I know when it's going to hurt to hear the words, yet I have to deliver the messages, and they're beautiful messages, just hard to listen to. Then, once the words are spoken, the happy memories and humor coming from the deceased start to replace the pain in the broken heart. It's necessary for healing, and it makes it possible for the grieving to rejoin the living.

# Mom and Dad

> It's interesting that when your heart breaks from losing someone, that even though it heals with a few scars, your heart seems to remember breaking every year in the days leading up to the anniversary of losing a loved one. The anxiety that starts to build knowing that day carried so much pain, is gripping.
>
> – Allison DuBois

I love that when I bring parents through, their version of heaven is usually centered around the time when their kids were little. They always reference their youngest child as 'baby'. It's really nice to know that we gave them some of their favorite days, some of the best days of their lives!

It's hard to lose a parent, the loss reduces you to a small child, no matter how many years you've lived. For many of us, the irony of life is that by the time we learn how to appreciate our parents, they die, and we're left with regret and sorrow. When a parent dies we instantly begin to reflect on our life with them and we start collecting in our mind the remnants of the last Christmas, last Father's Day or Mother's Day, our final mental snapshots with them., The ending moments when we realize we'll never get to make any more memories with them. The last time I laid eyes on my dad was Father's Day; kind of bittersweet, it's gone from a day that is exciting, to one that I sometimes dread.

The reason that I felt compelled to write this chapter is because I wanted to let younger people know that they need to make sure they take time out of their busy lives to spend with their parents. Tell your parents how much they mean to you, spend the money and take the time to go see them. Joe's dad passed in his sixties and my dad also passed in his 60s, neither of us knew what life would be like without them. Neither of us wanted to have to imagine that world, a less vivid one, a lonelier place to be. Nobody prepares young people for loss, because for most of them everything always feels so bright, full of color and possibilities. Life is still giving them gifts and hasn't begun taking them away yet.

It's a jolt to your soul, as you get older and you watch your own kids grow up and you recognize that they'll never remember your parents. Even harder because you often see so much of your parents' traits surface in your kids' energy and you want your kids to know how wonderful their grandparents were, but they'll only know about them through pictures and stories. For those of us who have lost a parent, or both, we look at adults who are walking with their parents and often we feel a little gypped, definitely envious. Sometimes we wonder why we didn't get to be that person, but as I know far too well, someone's got to draw the short stick, that's just part of life. I was very lucky to have my dad until I was 30, I have many memories of him, and he got to see all of his grandkids born, something that I sense that Joe wishes his dad had been here to witness. I mean, we know Jim is there, but Joe needed the physical nuances to reflect upon, a handshake, a hug, a smile, a 'Congratulations, son!' ... you know what I mean. So although we didn't have our dads for a long time, we had them long enough to know that we're luckier than many others were.

I see people at my events all the time who relate to me because they've also lost their dad. It makes me feel really good to be able to bring other 'kids' parents' through for them, I know how much it means. I know that one day our kids will lose Joe and I, I fear it for them, not us. Sometimes I write notes to them on the back of family photos in frames, so that when I'm dead I'll have something to work with, they'll find the right message exactly when they need it, I'll make sure that they do.

I live my life a little differently than most people, but you know what? I've learned from thousands of people who've lived and died, I'm listening to them because they know what they're talking about, they've been there done that! I'm a complex person, no doubt I'm not the easiest person to live with, because I gauge people's thoughts, and when they ask me what I'm thinking, I have to soften my answer, taking their fear that I might hear their thoughts into consideration. I also sometimes expect my family to know what I need, like I know what they need, it doesn't feel fair to have to tell them, they should just know. I can be such a big baby! I have to be responsible for so many people that sometimes it feels nice to be taken care of, too, but as my friend, astrologer Tom McMullan says, "Allison, you were born with great abilities, you don't get to be taken care of, get used to it." I know he's right, but if we can choose to come back in a next life, I think I'll be the damsel in distress instead it seems so much more romantic and requires far less energy. I guess 'the grass is always greener on the Otherside of the fence!' That's a little medium humor.

I've weighed what I've heard from the deceased with what I see the living doing, and they have an advantage over us through experience, but when the living doesn't listen to what they're trying to say, it only hurts us. They can only do so much, some living people are hell-bent on being unhappy, and nobody living or dead can do anything about that, it has to come from within the person choosing misery over having a memorable life. I see them every now and then, they're real life 'energy drains'. They'll take what you've got and then move on to the next energy source. I try to keep those people at a distance, because if I let them take too much of my energy, I don't have it for people who really need it. If a person's energy, and the thought of them literally exhausts you, maybe it's time to re-evaluate the relationship. Deciding whether or not to include a person in your life can be a complicated situation; for me, mutual loyalty is the core of friendship, and an equal energy exchange, so you're not the one doing all the work. The idea of mutual loyalty helps anchor me when I'm weighing the pro's and con's of keeping someone in my life or not. Life is short, and I intend to take the ride with others who like to sit in the front row of the roller-coaster and hold hands as we laugh our way through life together.

## Daddy's girl

Sometimes I bring the parent through for grown children, but when the kids are still very young the messages have to be relayed through an older family member. A good example of this, is a reading that struck me personally because it reminded me that I had my dad much longer than many children do. The reading started out for the widow, and extended to reach out to their small daughter.

I was truly touched by a reading that I conducted for a grieving widow named Sharon, who had lost her husband unexpectedly less than a year before. It's always hard to hear the pain in the voice of the person I'm reading, as they force themselves to swallow and they struggle to talk.

The first words shared by Sharon's deceased husband, Jordan, in her reading was 'Wonder Woman'—he said she could do it all and unfortunately now she had to. He said that 'Sharon wearing his ring', which she confirmed she was, and talked about the pictures under the palm trees and referenced Sharon getting married or honeymooning in Hawaii. I thought maybe this had to do with a future marriage, but Sharon explained that it was them in the pictures. They got married in Hawaii and honeymooned there. I told her that Jordan was sharing this because it's a version of his heaven and he wanted Sharon to know it.

Jordan highlighted the month of May: this tells me it's either a birthday or a passing. Sharon explained he died on May 22$^{nd}$ the year before. He said, 'I was disoriented when I died,' which she already knew.

He referred to Sharon as a 'nurse' and compared her to Florence Nightingale; at this, Sharon was silent for a moment and then she told me that she was, in fact, a nurse.

Jordan's personality came through strongly in the reading, telling me he had a lot of friends in the military and that he loved and respected them all: he was actually a marine, Sharon revealed later. There were some light moments, too: 'I can fix anything, I'm good with my hands,' Jordan said, causing Sharon to laugh and agree that he was very mechanically inclined. He also mentioned her 'new car', which brought more smiles as she confirmed she'd just bought a brand new one.

There was, however, a message that Jordan was very serious about. 'Tell her I got them,' he said, referring to their six-year-old daughter letting balloons go for him on the anniversary of his death.

After the reading, Sharon asked me if Jordan came through to their daughter after he died. I said, "Yes, many times. He probably told her it's gonna be okay."

Sharon seemed to take a big breath and release it with relief, then said, "That's exactly what my daughter said he told her."

## The deceased's perspective

There were other details that surfaced in the reading but what I thought was sweet was Jordan's desire to let his little girl know that the communication between them was real. Through balloons and whispers, he was talking to her and she was talking back. Jordan will always be Lauren's dad, he'll make sure that she doesn't forget that he's a part of her life, and that she's the best part of him. He'll patiently wait, protecting her and wrapping his arms around her when the world gets to be too much for her to take. He will always be with her because she's daddy's little girl, and even when she has silver in her hair, she will remain young in his eyes.

## A father's love and humor

I recently did a reading for a young woman named Nicole whose dad had died. He had a sense of humor, to say the least. He talked about details of his illness and his personality in general, he worked hard to connect with his daughter and let her know that she still has a father.

As wonderful as the reading was, though, what struck me about Nicole's dad the most was that he was attempting to not only connect with his daughter but he wanted to lighten the energy to lessen her sadness. So he cracked a joke and said, 'Tell your mom it's okay to move, she should, and she doesn't have to worry about leaving me behind because I'm built to travel!' Meaning, he can go wherever he wants, he's weightless, and ready and willing to follow her anywhere that will make her happy again. Nicole had a good laugh, as did I.

I was surprised by the funny message; it's rare that the deceased make a joke about something that's not connected to their previous life but rather about what they are now—that's so unusual! Needless to say, the reading went well and I learned yet another lesson: that the sense of humor of the deceased is intertwined in their spirit—a spirit that they are well aware is light and 'built to travel'!

### THE DECEASED'S PERSPECTIVE

When the deceased is able to make us laugh in a reading, or through a memory, our energy level matches their's, then they can communicate with us more easily. Nicole's father was most interested in raising his daughter's spirit, and letting her know that she wasn't 'orphaned', that she still has a father. He also seemed to be attempting to nudge his wife forward, so she wouldn't feel that staying in their house kept her close to him. He'll be nearby, wherever she goes, so staying or going makes no difference when it comes to them being together. I do understand, though, why the living have a tendency to want to stay in the same home. As we go through life, we leave our energy on every object that we touch in our home, and our laughter and tears leave an emotional energy charge hanging in the air that we can often still hear echo and then we cling to, savoring every moment with the deceased. Sometimes all the deceased can do is try to communicate with us through signs and dreams to make us feel secure in their love, that they won't leave us no matter where we are.

### MOM'S STILL HERE—KIM'S STORY

Kim's story is a gorgeous example of the circle of life and how often, the universe will send us somebody to love while another we love is slipping away. Many of you will be able to relate to her bitter sweet story, of loss and enlightenment.

When I was 37 weeks pregnant with my second child, my beautiful, vibrant, vivacious, 55-year-old mother was diagnosed with inoperable brain cancer, and we were told that she only had six weeks to live. This news was devastating and terrifying. Fortunately, even though she was undergoing radiotherapy treatment, she was able to be at the birth of our son Nicholas, and it was a joyful experience for us.

The cancer attacked her brain stem, so she quickly began losing her ability to cough, swallow, walk, talk and every other basic function. I had always heard of people 'dying of cancer' but to see it and experience it first-hand was agonizing. My amazing father cared for her at home for as long as he could, and my brothers and I worked in shifts to spoon-feed her, care for her, and entertain the myriad of visitors who arrived to say their final goodbyes. It was my mom who finally made the decision during the last week of her life that she should go to hospital. She passed away four days later at the palliative care unit (and might I add that the nurses and doctors who work in that unit are more angel than human, they are the most compassionate, caring people I have ever met).

My new baby son was three months old by this stage and my oldest son was three years. It was a time of tumultuous emotions for me; on one hand I was experiencing the wonderful joys of motherhood, and at the same time trying to grieve. With my husband working long hours, I slipped into a depression that was very hard to get myself out of. I tried talking to a counsellor but I didn't feel I got any benefit from it.

The only thing that helped was reading and re-reading the myriad of spiritual books that my mom had owned. She was a very spiritual woman, extremely outgoing and talkative and never, ever afraid to express her opinion on spiritual matters, whether she was talking to a minister or an atheist! She strongly believed that our spirit lives on after we die.

That same year I couldn't wait to get my hands on Allison DuBois' first book *Don't Kiss Them Goodbye*. I had always been a huge fan of the television show *Medium*, so I was looking forward to learning about the real Allison Dubois. I got so much comfort from reading Allison's book, her words resonated with me and I began to recall the conversations that I'd had with my mom about a 'knowingness' that she and I had experienced all our lives.

About two days before Mom died, we were all sitting in her hospital room and were talking about what it would be like on 'the other side' and how Mom could contact us to let us know she had arrived safely. Mom had always told us that when you see a white feather, this was someone in heaven trying to communicate with you. Even though Mom was unconscious, I told her that when she arrived in heaven she was to send us a white feather. Well, our mother was an excellent communicator in life and appears to be just as so in the afterlife.

A couple of days after her funeral, my three-year-old Nathaniel woke up and said, "Mommy! I had a dream about Nana and she was all better!" He also told me he could see Nana on the ceiling and that she could see him. He said, "Nana is in Greenland where it is all green, and she is looking after all the little babies."

A few weeks after her passing we were taking a family walk. Our baby Nicholas was in his baby carriage lying on his back. Suddenly a white feather came floating down towards us (it was just like in the movie Forrest Gump!) and landed right in the palm of Nicholas's hand in the baby carriage. It was one of those moments that if my husband and I hadn't seen it with our own eyes we wouldn't have believed it. I said, "Hello, Mom!" Since then white feathers appear in the most random of places, at times when I most need confirmation.

That was also the beginning of persistent, almost nightly lucid dreams where Mom was giving me messages and information. She would appear to me in a dream when I needed her most. She told me: 'You think I am gone, but I'm not, I am still a part of everything and everyone.' I had to keep a pen and notebook by my bed just to keep up with the messages. So cool! I felt like a whole new world had opened up to me.

In December 2010, I was very excited to be attending one of Allison's seminars in Sydney. I took my husband James (who was skeptical of psychic/mediums) and we had front-row seats so we were able to take everything in. Although I did not get read by Allison that night, I left the seminar on cloud nine; I was so buoyed up by the fantastic energy of the seminar and the audience connecting and supporting each other. (Side note: After seeing people's emotional reactions to Allison's readings of their deceased loved ones, my husband finally got off the fence and is now a staunch Allison Dubois supporter!)

Then, early in 2011, a few days after the sixth anniversary of Mom's death, I was lucky enough to have the opportunity to have a telephone reading with Allison—all the way from the other side of the world. I was amazed because I knew how long her waiting lists were and I was sure Mom must have arranged this from her side. We had the reading reserved but Allison got sick and her secretary called to say we would have to rearrange a date, but she wasn't sure when. The following Wednesday night I had a dream where Mom appeared to me and told me the reading would be rescheduled for 5 a.m. Friday. The next morning Allison's secretary called me to say the reading would be rescheduled for—you guessed it—5 a.m. Friday! Further proof to me that Mom was running this show!

    I hardly slept the night before the reading; I was so anxious and excited. One of the first things Allison told me was that Mom said she was still a wife, mother and grandmother, and that she was not ready to leave us, she was still around all the time. She told me Mom appeared immaculate and well-manicured, with long painted nails. This was proof that she was connecting with my mother because she was always extremely well-groomed; never leaving the house without full hair and makeup done, and she had the most beautiful long natural nails that were always painted in vivid colors. By comparison, my nails are ragged and bitten; I certainly don't take after her in the manicure department!

    Allison told me that Mom was glad she lived her life to the fullest and she didn't leave any loose ends. She laughingly added, "Boy, she talks a lot!" This was typical Mom; she was a confident conversationalist and was never known to be standoffish when meeting a new person. Allison said Mom was currently working through some issues with her deceased father (he passed away three days before my youngest son was born), and they had some problems that needed sorting out. This was news to me, but I later found out that the two of them had a lot of issues when Mom was a teenager that I had never known about.

Allison said, "She has your little white dog." I cried then! My little white Maltese, Muffy, had passed away aged sixteen just a couple of months prior to the reading.

She also had messages for my dad and my brothers, specifically to my middle brother who had found it very hard to cope with our mother dying. Mom said to tell him, 'It wasn't in the cards' for her to stay. This was specific to our mother, she had a lot of unusual sayings and this one she said all the time. Mom also wanted me to tell my eldest son Nathaniel that she had gotten his balloons. This was significant because just a few days prior we had released balloons at Mom's gravesite on her anniversary, and my son had written a letter addressed to 'Nana in Heaven' that we attached to the balloons.

Allison said Mom wished she was still able to cook so she could help me to get Nicholas to eat his vegetables (he is the fussiest eater!). Mom had been an amazing cook; her dishes were legendary amongst our family and friends.

There were many other connections and words specific to my mother. I was blown away that Allison was so spot-on. The experience was exactly like having a phone conversation with my mother; with Allison acting as the interpreter. Allison ended the reading by saying that Mom was pulling back her energy and sending lots of white feathers to me. I hung up the phone feeling like I was ten foot tall and bulletproof that day. The grief I had felt was eased immeasurably. I felt at peace. It was wonderful that Mom opened the doorway while she was living to teach us that the soul is forever, and to have that reiterated by Allison, with such detailed and clear confirmation; it's something that I will cherish forever. I am indebted to the amazing Mrs DuBois.

I still miss my mom, of course; no one loves you like your mother does! Sometimes when the world gets too much, I wish she was here to look after me, but I take great comfort in knowing with conviction that she is taking care of me and my family from her unique position on the other side of the veil.

I am so grateful to Allison for writing her books and sharing her exceptional and passionate outlook on life. I have all Allison's books (read and re-read)—they continue to be such a source of knowledge and comfort to me. Her practical advice for making the most of our time on earth inspires me daily to dizzy heights. I can honestly say Allison has inspired me to 'Live Life Large'. Thank you from the bottom of my heart.

## The deceased's perspective

Kim's mom Denise had a healthy outlook on life and death and she passed this on to her daughter. So when it came time for me to bring her mother through, it was easy because her energy was already so well adjusted. Denise wasn't just able to come through to me, she had already communicated with her grandchild to pass on comfort to her family. Denise touched a lot of people when she was alive and clearly she still had the desire to ease hearts and help her loved ones to grow spiritually. Denise was so very proud of her daughter for many reasons but, in that moment, her pride revolved around Kim's ability to stay connected to her.

## A mother's wisdom

I had the pleasure of reading a woman named Ginger, who was missing her mom and wanted me to bring her through. Her mother came through with a lot of energy, excited to be heard by her daughter. She pointed to her chest and said that when she was dying she found it impossible to breathe. Ginger understood, and told me that her mother had battled lung cancer, so her mom's description made perfect sense. I was amused that her mother showed me a picture of the beautiful actress Audrey Hepburn, making a comparison to herself as having similar energy. She was happy to be with her younger brother who had died tragically in his youth, and she also wanted Ginger to know that she wasn't alone. She mentioned being with 'Robert', too, and Ginger said that her mother had an unrequited love named Robert who had also died. I'm glad they found each other in death. I loved it when her mother mentioned a man for Ginger and told her to go to her high-school reunion. Ginger was surprised by this because her high-school reunion was the following week. This is one of those situations where the deceased can only do so much; they can give us advice but it's up to us to take it!

### Ginger's story

My mother was a big personality when she lived. In many ways, she was bigger than her environment and era would allow her to be—she was a feminist before it was 'allowed'; she was brilliant in a time when women did not excel intellectually; she was funny, clever, loved to laugh and party. Her naturally free spirit was consistently frowned upon in her era, and therefore she was never fully realized as an independent woman. Her escapades, while challenging for her two daughters and her family, were her way of rebelling; she was just trying to express herself, her authentic personality. She was an enigma her entire life—she tried to conform to the morals and mores of the time, but in doing so she was left empty and unfulfilled in many ways. To combat the chronic depression that resulted, she drank excessively and she was addicted to men and pills.

I say all of this with tremendous love and respect for her. Yes, she was my mother. But she was also a woman, a human being, with human frailties. As an adult mother myself, I can empathize with her in many ways. It is through her that I learned to laugh from my belly, to quench my insatiable thirst for knowledge, to love with passion and abandonment, and to pursue my dreams. Thankfully, with the help of great friends and a great therapist, I have been able to assimilate all my mother's experiences, choices and challenges into lessons that inform me as a mother, and a woman.

My mother came through in the reading chatting and laughing; she started talking mid-sentence. This was my mother, the life of the party! Everyone who knew her loved her. She had a magnetic personality; it was her lack of discretion which caused the trouble.

She then said that she and I are a lot alike—same energies, only the positive traits she said. Then my mother touched the ring on her hand; I have that ring, she left it for me. It is a beautiful sapphire and diamond ring, an antique piece.

My mom showed Allison a vision of her around the time that

she died, she said she was having trouble breathing—in fact, she died of lung cancer. She said in the reading that she never wanted to be a burden for any of us—that was so important for her. My mom was fiercely independent, and she would say to us over and over, "I don't want to worry anyone. I don't want my girls to have to take care of me."

Allison mentioned 'Lynn' as a middle name connection—my mom's full name was Rosalyn Jean. The 'lyn' is definitely middle!

My mom told me, 'Sorry for the mess.' This could be interpreted several ways—her life was a mess, as she called it. And we were constantly cleaning up for her—when she was an active alcoholic, the messes were real and tangible. As she grew older and continued to make poor decisions, I was straightening things out for her, helping her out of sticky situations.

My mom's book reference was huge, she mentioned how much she liked to read—she read constantly, as do I. She read the World Book encyclopedia set three times when I was in high school. She was a voracious reader and I do the same.

In the reading my mom said that she reverted to the age of 24. That was the age she was when her brother killed himself. That was the moment things really turned for her, so it seems she went back to the days when he was still alive. She had felt guilty about his suicide, and she started to drink, and cavort. She neglected us as a result and we grew up fending for ourselves. Sad and lost, she never recovered from the hurt from the loss of her brother.

When my mom said, 'I am with the uncle,' I instinctively knew she meant her brother, my Uncle Hilary. Since, he was the one who killed himself when she was 24 and I was five. My Uncle

Hilary's death was a large part of why my mother started to drink and mentally 'check-out'.

I immediately recognized the Robert connection to my mom that Allison spoke of. This man was one of the many 'loves' of her life; there were many men, but Robert came in and out of our lives several times. He played the role of hero for her, they had an unrequited situation, they never could work things out. But I believe she loved him more than any of the others.

In the reading my mom was holding up a bottle of pills and throwing it away—this made sense because my mom was addicted to Xanax just before she became sober. Her final attempt to commit suicide involved taking 100 pills and drinking two-fifths of a bottle of vodka. We found her, and had her committed to 72-hour lockup. Upon release, she went into rehab and was clean/sober from then until her death eight years later. Even in these struggles she was an amazing woman. Her determination proved to be what saved her life; the last eight years saved all our lives, really—gave my sister and me the chance to get to know her finally, and my daughter the opportunity to know the best of her grand-mamma.

Allison told me that my mom said that she always wanted to live in California—you have no idea how spot on this is. For my entire childhood, she would tell us that we were going to move to California, that she belonged in California, that we were going to live there. Circumstances never presented themselves for her to do so, but when I turned eighteen and decided to go to college, I applied to California schools. I was accepted at UCLA and Chapman University. I attended Chapman in Orange, California. My sister followed me the next year. When my mom retired from

Dupont after 33 years, she moved to California to be with us. It took us a while but her dream finally came true.

My mom spoke about my 'father' in the reading—she said he was standing silent beside her. His mouth was covered. "Something is not right," Allison said. "He couldn't take it. He was imbalanced, things were out of balance. He was disconnected and he felt numb." In fact, my mother and father had a tumultuous relationship. Volatile and transient, they married and divorced twice. My father left my mother when she announced that she was pregnant with me; he doubted (as did the rest of the family) that he was my father. When I was born, he returned and he tried to be my father. He tried to do the right thing. My mother vilified him, made him out to be a villain. He wasn't. He was just uneducated, he tried to do the right thing and he was unfulfilled in his life as well.

Allison said that, "Frank was standing next to my dad"—family folklore says that my real father may have been one of four possible boyfriends at the time, one of them was named Frank. (I will dig more into this with my relations.)

Allison said that my mom lit a candle on a cake, indicating a major birthday taking place; my daughter Eve turned sixteen the week prior to the reading. Mama said she was with Eve. She spoke about Eve—worried about the company she keeps—boys are dangerous! My mom wanted me to tell Eve, 'She is with her when she goes to Disneyland.' Eve was just at Disneyland the week before; she goes frequently. It is the quintessential California place, and Mama is there with her.

She said that she knows that I am writing a book—she said it's called 'A love letter to mom'—it is about her and my life growing up. She is the one who brings me the ideas to write. When I get writer's block, Allison said for me to ask my mother to bring me the ideas. (I will do this!)

There are still things of hers that we haven't found/gone through yet. Still pictures to find. My mom told me to not give away her 'unmentionables'; just to throw them away. Still a Southern Lady even now!

Allison said there was a camera in my mom's hand—she said there are still pictures that I haven't developed that we will find.

My mom mentioned my high-school reunion, she said I needed to go. The reunion was the weekend following the reading! I couldn't get away because of commitments with Eve. But mom said she was pushing a man to me, she wants me to be happy and to have someone who will take care of me.

Mom said that she has long hair now, that people always told her she was a 'natural beauty'. She used to tell us that all the time!

My final question was related to a business dream I have been working on. She told me to 'jump in with both feet—that I will know the right direction'.

Her final words to me still ring in my ear—'You kiss that pretty girl for me and tell her that I love her.' The cadence and soft Southern lilt inherent in these words ring so true about her.

She used to say that all the time—they are her words.

Finally, my mother said that she is with me every day. I am grateful for that. She is my inspiration, both in life and in death. She has always been life for me and the fact that she is happy now, truly happy, makes my life feel fuller and happier than ever. My daughter and I feel her every day. She is our North Star; she was frail, vulnerable, human, brilliant and an amazing light. That was true even during the challenging times.

### THE DECEASED'S PERSPECTIVE

Ginger's mom's motivation seemed to be fueled by her desire to see her daughter in a happy relationship with a man. She kept stressing that 'she didn't want her to be alone'. I believe this feeling stemmed from her mother missing out on Robert while alive, something she's making up for now. Ginger's mom has a romantic heart and she wants her daughter to feel special and loved, safe in the arms of the one she loves. It also seemed crucial for her mother to let Ginger know that she didn't have to worry about her being alone in her heaven.

Deceased moms and dads are *still* parents, they continue to love us and guide us. They will spiritually knock on our door until we answer them and acknowledge their presence. Their motivation in reaching us is to remind us to not feel like orphans but rather to embrace the unbreakable bond between parent and child.

### PARENTS ARE FOREVER

I conducted a very special reading for a woman named Mina, who had three people she wanted to hear from. I'm writing about her reading in this chapter because her parents are taking care of Mina's son on the Otherside, and I think it's important to illustrate the connection between our loved ones who pass, and how they come together for us. I brought Mina's son Lonnie through first, but it was his grandparents who lent him their energy so that he could touch Mina completely by coming through to her in as powerful a way as possible, and that's incredibly special. When the dead join forces to be heard, it's done out of their unwavering love for us. Lonnie was able to come through at the beginning of the reading because of the assistance of his grandparents. Mina's mom and dad knew that she needed to hear from her son more than she needed to hear from them. They were willing to wait to speak to Mina and they put Mina's needs first because she's their child, just like Lonnie is Mina's child.

Lonnie did a solid job coming through for his mom; he was funny, kind of sly, and sarcastic. He let his mother know that he reverted to being a teenager again and then he picked up a piece of pizza and took a large bite out of it. Lonnie said that at the moment he died he was confused, not himself, and numb. He said he spends a lot of time around his sister. He mentioned that one of his signs is the music that he plays for his family. When Lonnie talked about his friends all wearing 'his shirt', this confused me a little, but Mina explained that after he died, his friends had T-shirts made for Lonnie with his name and photo on them. They wore 'his shirt' as a memorial to him. Lonnie also said that he really liked Las Vegas, and he'd been there since he had died, with his family. This showed Mina that he was still very much part of her every day life, enjoying her adventures along side of her.

After Lonnie, Mina's mom finally had her turn. She said that Mina will always be eight years old to her. Her mom laughed about their jewelery size being different, and Mina explained that her mom's rings didn't fit her. She assured Mina that she would be fine, and that she was taking care of her precious boy. Mina's mother said, 'She loved Mina so much that she wished she could put her in her heart and carry her around with her so that nothing could ever hurt her again.'

Then I brought through Mina's dad, who lovingly talked about his 'two girls and boy', which were Mina and her siblings, and said all of the things that he needed to say to Mina. He also joked that it was his piercing eyes that really grabbed his wife's attention when they were courting! Apparently, Mina's dad had blue eyes and dark hair so he would have been known for his eyes. He talked about dying with a full head of hair; he was proud of that fact. Mina laughed and confirmed this to be true.

### The deceased's perspective

Lonnie and his grandparents' intention was to let Mina know that she's not alone in her life. They were stepping in to support her, love her and be present. They chose their words carefully, they doled out their memories of Mina for me to relay to her, letting her know that she's included in their versions of heaven, and an active love in their existence. Through Lonnie's eyes I could see how he worries about his mom, and also how he sees her on a daily basis. He showed his mom looking off in the distance, searching for him with her heart, as he stood next to her trying to assure her that he's still there. Mina's parents walk alongside their grandson in spirit, sharing smiles and laughter. They also stand in front of their daughter, helping her to move forward in life by holding her hands and encouraging her to take small steps. Until the day comes that she joins them and her heart will no longer have to search for the ones that she thinks she lost.

* * *

All of these readings are examples of the unbreakable bonds formed between parents and their children. Our parents' voices are among the very first that we ever hear as a baby and they soothe us. Hearing the words from your parents after they pass has the same effect on us, it soothes us. If you keep an open mind and you listen with your heart, the conversations with your parents can continue forever.

The next time that you miss your parents, keep in mind that they have a spectrum of ways to help you to get through their death. I believe that we're sent the people that we need, when we need them, by our deceased loved ones. I feel like they orchestrate the relationships on our behalf. After my dad passed away, I was sent a sort of surrogate dad. He was someone that my dad actually knew of because he was a television personality in Arizona for many years. I met him while on a press tour for my television show Medium. I had watched him on TV my whole childhood and then I actually got to grow up to be his friend. Our kids love him and his wife very much, we all do. I believe that my dad has helped to bring many fantastic people into my life to help patch the wound visited upon my heart the day that he died.

Tell the Otherside what you need. If you've lost someone, maybe you can find a little comfort in another wonderful person, too; you're not replacing your loved one, just opening your heart to a new friendship.

# Pets are family

Since I first began reading people, and bringing through the deceased, pets have appeared with the deceased. Anything that you loved, that was alive, has the ability to wait for you, and they usually wait with a family member of yours, who preceded you in death. When I do readings, I often have dads coming through saying, 'Tell my daughter, I have her damn cats.' I think it's funny that they love us enough to keep our pets for us until we get to the Otherside, but they're not always as fond of our animals as we are; some are, and some aren't. Either way, they do it for us because they love us, and they don't like to see us sad, so anything that we loved, they now take care of as well, with all of the love that we did.

Your pets who have passed away are also able to roam your house, and lay in their favorite spots, as well as interact with any of your living pets. I talk about this later in the chapter, and Mack's story is the perfect example of how deceased pets set up a 'pecking order' and how the new pet respects their seniority.

I've also noticed that, much like people who die in threes or a few all around the same time, animals do, too! It's like cosmically, a burst of energy comes into the world and pulls at the souls of those who are barely hanging on to their bodies. Recently, I hugged my friend Adrianne the week her beautiful Maine Coon cat, Sergeant Pepper, passed away. She had lost her closest feline friend and I could feel her broken heart struggle to move forward in life. There was something about that cat, he looked at her as though he could read her thoughts, and he just 'knew' when she needed him. So, Sergeant Pepper started the roll call to heaven. That same week my friend Draden lost his little hedgehog, Squirt, who had been born in my house while Draden was house-sitting for us. Quite a surprise for me, to return home to baby hedgehogs! That little guy could fit in the palm of Draden's hand, but he was a mighty personality indeed! No matter how small a pet is, they usually have similar personalities to their owners, their 'adopted parents'. Draden's a character and Squirt was just as sassy! A lot of love was shared between the two of them, Draden took his buddy everywhere he went.

Around the same time, my friend Jen lost her bulldog Mack; he was so adorable and he loved Jen more than anything. She dressed him up for the holidays, and just seeing pictures of Mack in his many costumes lightened the hearts of all who appreciated his silly side. I wanted to put a derby hat on his head and stick a cigar in the corner of his mouth, so he'd look like a bootlegger! He lived being adored by Jen and she gave him the best life that any pet could ever ask for. Mack, Squirt and Sergeant Pepper—in fact, all very different animals—were similar because they were all loved and will live on in the hearts of the people who loved them.

Here's a short story from Jen about Mack and her new dog Sully: her beloved Mack had passed away unexpectedly. Sully, was her new Bulldog rescue, Jen wasn't sure how she'd move on from Mack but she knew that she had a lot of love to give. How would Mack feel about a new puppy cuddling with his mama?

### Jen's story

As soon as I took Sully in the building, he took off running down the hall, passed about eight doors and went straight to my door. It felt like Mack was showing him where his new home was. I was even more amazed when I took Sully out of the apartment for the first time and as soon as we exited my door, he knew to go right then which door was the emergency exit that leads to the outside where the grass is. Each time he's out there (every few hours), he knows exactly where the door is and the route back to my apartment. It's as if it's Mack. Truly amazing how Sully could even know this.

I feel Mack's energy here in the apartment and have caught Sully running like crazy after nothing at all, zipping under the table and around the house. Another thing, I've watched and he will not lay in any of Mack's favorite spots. He chose not to sleep in my room last night and slept next to the couch in the living room on the opposite side of where Mack would lay.

## THE IMPORTANCE OF PETS

Pets are souls sent to us to teach us something, and to love us when people don't realize we need it; or they are sent to us because sometimes we only let our guard down for a soul who doesn't judge us. We can't always say that of the people in our lives; maybe those reasons, and more.

Some people don't understand why pet lovers get so upset when they lose their companions, but I get it. Animals communicate with us through their hearts and souls, not just their mouths like many people do. Pets won't tell you that they love you and then hurt you. Often, people aren't able to connect to other people with their whole heart since their heart has been mishandled before. Animals love you unconditionally and won't disappoint you, they feel safe to those who've been hurt by the people in their life. Pets are very good at filling an emotional void in anyone.

I have a very close friend who I'll call 'Ann', she's one of those warrior souls who fights for the good of the people and asks nothing in return. Her cat was really like a family member to her, one that soothed her after a hard day's work, day after day, for years. She represented a safety zone to Ann after she got home from dealing with violent criminals all day. I knew this cat and she only, and I mean *only*, liked Ann and her husband—she was extremely territorial. If you approached her cat, she swiftly let you know to back off and that she was not the kind of cat, who would love on just anybody. Probably because the cat knew she had to protect the hearts of her owners, and keep the castle safe. I always knew that if someone came in their house unwelcome, that cat would've taken plenty of DNA from the burglar. She was a tough cat! I really loved that this loyal friend was there for Ann the year she lost her mother, whom Ann idolized, then the next year after Ann lost her sister unexpectedly, the cat never left Ann's side. If Ann was home the cat was checking on her and showing her love. Unfortunately, recently, Ann's cat passed away, and my friend was, and I think still is, devastated.

So animal lovers come from all walks of life. I know that police officers tend to be very close to their animals, especially the ones who work with police dogs. They deal with people who act savage all day so when they go home it's nice to see the soft side of life and hang out with their loyal pet.

Pets are even used in the United States to help reform non-violent inmates by teaching them how to take responsibility for caring for another. For example, in one program I know of, if the inmate takes good care of their pet and displays good behavior, they get to take their buddy home with them when they've completed their sentence. I've watched videos of the inmates with their pets and it's actually quite moving how much love is there, and how transformed for the better the inmates become.

Animals teach us empathy for others, and they love us unconditionally. My cat Daisy Mae lays with me when I'm sick in bed, and we share Saltines.

I think that if every lonely person adopted a pet to love, our world would be a much sweeter place. We've rescued three cats: one was thrown over a backyard fence, one was tossed in a trash can, and one was left to me by a dying friend, a sad scenario that couldn't be helped. Thank you to all of the people who rescue animals and work to protect them.

If you're feeling lonely, check out a pet shelter near you; your life will feel more meaningful by the minute!

### Our cat Caesar

When my friend Domini died in 2002, we adopted one of the kittens in her apartment. We named him Caesar and he was an orange tabby. A pretty cat, he had white paws and it looked like his whiskers sprouted out of two big, white cotton balls. He was a loving kitty, but he spent ten years battling bad kidneys. We tried everything the vet told us to, including Prozac and prescription cat food. His kidneys had gotten so bad by 2014, he always had a kind of pained look on his face. He had also started to not seem to know who we were sometimes. My friend Charlotte had just died, and now we were faced with Caesar dying. Some years just carry death energy. Caesar was my last and final connection to Domini, it was a strange feeling.

But Caesar was our little buddy and we couldn't watch him suffer any more. The girls said their tearful goodbyes, I was a wreck, and Joe was incredibly sad. This was a crushing moment for us all. Joe and I took Caesar to our vet, Dr. Samuelson, who is one of the most sensitive and comforting veterinarians I've ever met. I waited in the lobby, I couldn't bear it. Joe was the strong one, he went in and comforted our Caesar, told him we loved him and stayed until the end. While sobbing, I felt a sense of peace wash over me, as though everything was okay now. My eyes stopped tearing, my jaw relaxed and my heart lightened. I knew it was the moment that Caesar passed, and he was letting me know that he was better now, that he would be just fine. The door opened and Joe walked out and we went home in silence.

I know in my heart that Caesar's still with us, that he will always be a part of our family and that he'll be around throughout our lives. But we miss him like crazy, his weird meow, and how he nibbled on our fingers when we patted him. I know he's waiting for us. I joke with my father, 'Hey, Dad, here's another one for you to take care of until I get there! He's a special boy!'

Caesar had a lot of love to give, and we were lucky to have him with us as long as we did. Now, though, he is free of the body that hurt him so much, and I feel like he can now roam with his family and mine.

### Pets who see spirits

I often bring through spirits who feel bad because they've affected the pets of their living loved ones without meaning to cause trouble. A common scenario is when our deceased loved ones are trying to let us know that they are around, and so our pet responds by barking or reacting playfully but then gets scolded for it. Think of all of the pets who get tossed outside for their reaction to the presence of spirit energy! Often dogs bark to let you know that something else is present in the room. Many owners have sleeping babies or are sleeping themselves and are less than pleased by the barking.

Animals have a heightened sixth sense so their interaction

with spirits is quite common. Living pets will also react to the spirits of deceased pets who came before them: for example, they won't lay in the spot that belonged to the pets who have passed, because their spirits are still staking their claim and still inhabit those areas. You've got to admire the new pets who come in with big shoes to fill when their new owner adopts them after losing a cherished pet. Eventually, though, all pets end up together on the Otherside, and they already know each other from years of interaction since their veil is almost non-existent!

## Pets on the Otherside

I bring through pets in readings very frequently, but only sometimes do I get a name. Once I brought through a dog whose name was 'Rufus' but I got his name as 'Brutus'—that was the closest I could get on that one! But with or without a name, pets appear in readings, making their presence known, because they love us and are so connected to us. Pets have often shown me what they look like, sometimes a name emerges in a reading and they usually show me where they liked to sleep or, how they felt when they were sick.

Animals who've passed look at the new living pet in their family with affection, they feel connected to them because they both love you. So don't feel guilty if you want a new pet after yours dies, it's actually a good thing, because a new pet brings vibrant life to your household for you and for the pet who remains in spirit.

When our pets die, they revert to a more youthful age, or the age that they were the happiest, just like human beings do. They split their time between being a companion to one of your deceased loved ones and still hanging out with you. They like to make sure you're okay, and they still get all of the care and cuddling that they need, usually from someone close to you. Pets who were sick or injured that have to be put to sleep know you were only releasing them from their pain, so try not to carry guilt if you had to make that heartbreaking decision. They understand more than we think, both in life and from the Otherside.

# *It's never too late*

### <u>HEALING THE WOUNDS BETWEEN THE LIVING AND THE DECEASED</u>

*I* cannot tell you how many stories of regret I hear from both the living and the dead—yes, I said the dead. The living's regret sometimes centers around them not being there when their loved one passed away. The deceased, though, always say that they were never alone, because their family and friends on the Otherside had come for them, and they want us to know that they weren't alone, or afraid, for even one moment.

Many of the people I've brought through tell me that while they were in the hospital dying, they held on for their living family to visit. They go on to say that once their husband and/or children—whomever needed them—finally leave them alone on their death bed, they let go and can finally drift away to join family and friends on the Otherside. I find it quite interesting that many of the dying can only let go when the ones they love leave the room, because something deep inside of them needs to hold on to the connection. They need to hold on for us. The living think that, somehow, they let their loved one down by not being there; in fact, they love you so much that sometimes they can only let go if they can no longer feel your presence. Otherwise they can't help but try to hold on, even when you keep telling them that it's okay to 'let go'.

Another common scenario of regret is when a deceased person was estranged from their loved one, and now the living wish they'd tried to reach out or at least spoken their peace before this person died. This usually applies to living children who were estranged from their parents, but not always. The problem with estrangement is that it's usually fueled by stubbornness; the exception is that sometimes the damage is too severe, such as with molestation or child abuse. Most of the time, though, estrangement involves people who don't even remember why they stopped talking in the first place. Or, once they say what divided their family out loud, it sounds so trivial that they see how silly it all was, because the fight paled in comparison to the finality of death. This applies to the regret of both the living and the deceased, they feel equally guilty. Whether they were in the right or not, it doesn't matter any more because the feud is now over. The finality of death has a way of putting things in to perspective.

We can't all agree on everything and that's okay. If people could learn to put their differences aside, and not carry the torch of resentment passed down from prior generations, then more families could live happily and without regret.

## Dead wrong

The deceased have regrets, obviously not for missing someone's passing, but rather missing someone's life. Sometimes death has a way of removing personal issues and matters of the mind, and in death your heart and soul expand. You will no longer care about what size house you have, taxes, or a fight with someone you love that turned into fifteen years of not speaking to one another and you can't remember why. When you're dead you will just want to let people who were in your life know that they were important to you. The deceased with regrets often say, 'I would do things better now, I didn't know that you needed me so much and I'm sorry that I wasn't there for you.' Or they say, 'I'm sorry I was wrapped up in my own life, and I wasn't thinking about what you needed.'

Sometimes they acknowledge that their issues in life and, often their bad habits, started in childhood, and they're sorry for being emotionally unavailable. Frequently those with such issues say that they didn't feel worthy of being loved.

The regretful deceased often ask for forgiveness, and they want the living to know that they have lighter energy now, and they would like to be able to move forward to being a positive part of our lives. The deceased usually say that they feel more alive now, more than they ever had in their actual life, and they almost seem excited to be able to help the living.

## HEALING AFTER SUICIDE

I talk in detail about suicide in Chapter 7, but here I want to focus on healing after a loved one has been lost in this way. Since this chapter focuses on healing 'after' someone has passed, it's essential to include suicide because it's the type of passing that involves the most severe regret. The pain is monumental for the living and the dead, as both sides still struggle with the loss being at the hands of the very person who's missed. When you lose someone to suicide, it creates a complicated array of emotions; you miss them and are kind of mad at them at the same time. The living feel like the deceased must not have loved them, otherwise they wouldn't be able to leave them behind, or that their love wasn't enough to keep them here. What I hear the deceased say in readings is that either they felt like their family would be better off without them, or the pain inside of them that they woke up with every day was so severe that they didn't see any other way to overcome it.

Parents who commit suicide seem to regret it the most, because they feel they let their kids down and changed their lives forever—literally changed who their children are by dropping out of their life. Their children, however, are also a big part of the reason that the parent hung on as long as they did; parents who died from suicide tell me this frequently. I feel such deep empathy for kids who lose a parent to suicide, because even when I bring their parent through in a reading, the apology can only go so far—the fact is, their parent made a conscious decision to leave them, something parents promise they'll never do. Parents who die at their own hands do still truly love their children, and the remorse they feel, watching their family struggle to understand why they did what they did, is almost more than they can bear. This is a deep wound to heal, but it's important to try, in order to live a peaceful life.

For the people who have lost a loved one to suicide, please keep in mind that their death occurred at a time that they weren't in their right mind. It had nothing to do with their love for you: it was a combination of a chemical imbalance, depression and sometimes alcohol and/or drugs, a recipe for disaster. Never question what you mean to them, you most likely play a starring role in their versions of heaven. If you can get your mind around the intense pain that they must have felt to end their life so drastically, maybe you can find it in your heart to forgive them. Invite them back into your life, talk to them, their energy is calm and content now, and probably quite a bit younger! Once you've established a new relationship, you can both start moving forward together. By doing this, both of you can thrive, evolve, and be at peace with your existence together.

# Communicating with the dead

> You have a choice, listen to the dead with your ears and hear nothing, or listen to them with your heart and have a conversation.
>
> – Allison DuBois

## REMOVING YOUR EMOTIONAL WALL

*B*efore I go into how you can communicate with the dead, I'd like to address pain, because it can prevent you from hearing spirits. Sometimes the pain stems from worrying about their suffering around the time of their death. People who die in car accidents are a good example for this lesson. When a person is in an accident, spirits usually surround them and 'remove' them from their body so they can't feel the pain. When I bring through people who died in car accidents, they often say that they were numb, and couldn't feel the trauma; that's because the entities around them are buffering their pain and fear. When a living loved one can only think of the moments surrounding a death, they trap themselves in that moment, while the person who died has already moved past it. So, for the sake of being able to communicate with spirits, try not to focus on the actual death, otherwise you're setting yourself up for failure to communicate. If they can't communicate with you, those who've passed on will go through your living family and friends in order to reach you. Don't think they don't care about you, and are going to everyone but you; you are just not accessible to them at this time. When you reach a point in your grief where you're truly ready to communicate with them, it needs to occur through an open heart and the desire to share your life with them. Communication is very hard when you try and do it through desperation. The deceased need a high energy frequency to connect to, and that's usually by sharing a happy memory with you and/or through your ability to celebrate their life.

The reason that so many people 'dream' about their deceased loved ones is because when you're asleep, you're easier to access. When you're awake your mind has more of a tendency to dismiss the signs that they give you, even if you don't mean to do so. If you dream about them, they're trying to communicate with you, so thank them for the 'visit' and begin to build a new spiritual relationship with them. They want to remain a part of your life, and in order to make this happen, you have to help them, by not only talking to them but by continuing to share moments with them. Let them show you how to live again!

Talking to deceased loved ones is a conversation that most people would love to have, and they search the depths of their soul trying to hear their loved one's voice. Some people even imagine calling their loved one on a phone with a curly cord, just like how their mom was always on the phone gabbing on while making dinner for them as a child. The desire to communicate is there, the grieving can usually visualize how the conversation would look or sound. When the bereaved can't get through their emotional block built from their pain, they try other outlets like mediums, because we can communicate with the deceased but aren't personally involved in an overly vulnerable way. But much like Dorothy's red slippers in the *Wizard of Oz*, your ability to go home was there all along, you just have to believe, and learn how to use what you've already been given.

### BE CAREFUL WHAT YOU WISH FOR...

People often tell me that they wish they had my same abilities —well, the beauty of the gift comes with a price. For example, every time I fly on a plane, the turbulence unravels me; this is because turbulence reminds me of the feeling that pilots get when they fall from the sky. I've brought through many pilots and soldiers who died in airplane and helicopter crashes, and I carry that with me. Although I experience only a fraction of what the deceased actually felt at the time they died, it still affects my life. I wouldn't relinquish my gift for anything but make no mistake, it rapidly ages you!

In order to head-tap people like I do when I get into the heads of criminals, you have to be very 'turned up' energetically; this also makes everything around you sort of annoying. Sounds are amplified, people's energy can literally knock you over, and you feel like everyone's invading your space. Another reason why flying on airplanes isn't my favorite thing is because people literally do affect you, whether you're sitting down and someone has their rear-end in your face, or the guy behind you unapologetically uses the back of your chair as his personal stretching post and you as leverage. You all know what kind of people I speak of, the ones who are unaware that anyone else in the world exists but them. As I write this, I have a guy behind me just like that; if you add alcohol to him you'd have a super special kind of ... well, you get the point.

There are pro's and con's to everything, and being able to read energy is an amazing gift, but it also extends to people's energy that you'd rather not know. As you evolve spiritually, you will become more vulnerable to everything around you—it is, what it is! Just *breathe*.

People who have 'healer' energy will pick up on other's ailments; a cough can send you through the roof, or someone's lung cancer can steal your breath. Empaths have to be particularly careful not to hold on to all the illness around them, otherwise it can make them very sick and they will not only take on the symptoms, but holding on to the energy can allow it to manifest in their own systems. As long as healers visualize the illness washing off them and going down the drain away from them, or any exercise that removes the tainted energy from their body, they should be just fine. Healers absorb so much painful energy, I don't know how they do it, but then they tell me that they don't know how I can 'talk to the dead', so there you go. Spiritual people empathize with one another, that's what we do, and it's nice to roam the earth with others who 'do the work'.

Keep in mind that having a gift comes with a price, one worth paying in my opinion, but we do encounter a lot of trauma as we go down a path to help others to rejoin the living. Spiritual people don't just pick up on grandparents who died naturally. You will experience suicides, murders, accident victims, babies dying, people who were in the wrong place at the wrong time, and a hundred other types of death. So if you honestly want to strengthen your ability to communicate with the dead then be prepared to feel pain in order to hear the deceased and you will have to learn to control it. Otherwise, feeling too much, will take you a part. If you're up to the challenge, and you want to learn about setting up boundaries between you and the dead, then start with Basic Mediumship. Be prepared, to alter your life through an adjusted lifestyle and to live in a very deep way. Your friends will be shuffled, as new friends come in and a few old ones go out because some won't understand your desire to learn this new language! It's called *evolution* don't be afraid of it, I find the dead to be more fun than most of the living. They live in an amazing world full of light, a true kaleidoscope of memories and times long past.

## BASIC MEDIUMSHIP ADVICE

Being relaxed and in a healthy state of mind is especially important when it comes to using your abilities. If you're distracted by kids and work, or obsessing over your past, you're not going to get clear information. When I prepare for a reading, I always light a white candle and focus on the glow of the candle. I also do some deep-breathing exercises that help put me in a clear, focused frame of mind, and it elevates my energy to connect with spirit. I also close the doors leading to other rooms, it seems to keep the energy around me, and my readings just feel more focused.

I find visualizing a bright light growing inside of me, and then extending outside of me, seems to act as a sort of beacon to the Otherside that I have strong, open energy waiting to connect with them. You can't be distracted, so you want to be in a quiet place while concentrating on connecting. If you want the opposite effect and you want to block the Otherside, then playing music can help you achieve that goal. Any amount of noise will shut down hearing the Otherside when you desire quiet.

To further open up, tell someone related to you who's on the Otherside to work with you on recognizing signs. This would involve them giving you signs to interpret for practice, beginning a clear relationship with the deceased to move forward on the same energetic page. It's like allowing them to hold your hand and plug into your energy, just as you've now plugged into theirs. You can also educate yourself by using photos of the deceased as a tool to connect with the person. Often a physical image will conjure up a stronger sense within you, opening a door in your mind where you start feeling what their personality is, and begin to have pictures flash through your mind from that person's life experiences.

A photograph will also make the deceased feel a connection

or give them a 'way in' to the person gazing at their image. This puts you on the same energetic page as the deceased, because both the deceased and the person holding their image are focused on each other in that moment. Write down any impressions you get while holding the photograph; it helps to bring focus when learning how to 'read' people and energies.

Some mediums use objects that belonged to the deceased, and this practice is called 'psychometry'. Sometimes objects that carry the energy of the deceased can make it easier to 'dial in' to the entity that you wish to communicate with, due to the fact that it mattered to the deceased in both life and death. Usually, because the object connected them to somebody they love and was symbolic of their relationship, this can often be 'felt' when you hold the artifact.

There are lots of various ways to strengthen the many facets of your abilities. Remember, they are limitless, and you are limitless when it comes to being strong enough to connect and predict. Continuing to practice is key, as well as being in the right head-space to receive clear, precise information through your senses. Whether you do pilates, yoga, paint, play a musical instrument or golf, whatever relaxes you will only make you better at performing strong enough to achieve 20/20 vision with your 'third eye'.

### INTERMEDIATE MEDIUMSHIP ADVICE

Once you grasp the basics, learning how to centre yourself and connect with spirit, then it's time to understand how information will come to you. When a spirit is trying to communicate with you, they will flash pictures through your mind to convey moments of their life. I find these visuals incredibly helpful when trying to distinguish a car they drove, or what they looked like. Sometimes they're wearing a uniform, and then you know they were military, or a police officer, etc. I've had women show me pictures of them as a beauty queen, riding in the back of a car in their hometown parade! Visuals are very cool.

Another form of communication comes via flashing words through your mind; names are often given to you this way, or they'll be whispered in your ear. You know if the deceased yell something in your ear that they have a lot of emotion behind the message, and if you're doing a professional reading or arranged reading, then make sure to convey it, or they won't let up on that piece of information. If a random stranger has a spirit connected to them who's doing this to you, write down what they yelled on a piece of paper then burn the paper.

It is unethical for a medium to convey information to a person who didn't ask for a reading—that's called 'ambush-reading'. Ambush-reading people is not okay, even though there are television shows that do this. It's as unfair to do to others as it is for someone to bully you or demand a reading from you when you're enjoying your personal time.

Boundaries are incredibly important, so make sure you have clear boundaries, with both the living and the deceased. There's a time and a place for readings, and they're best done in a quiet place, and with mutual respect. Don't ever feel like you have to prove anything to anyone in order to be validated, as long as you believe in yourself, and in the afterlife, that's the core part of you that counts the most, and you'll be just fine.

Sometimes, the deceased communicate through smell; perfume, cigars, food and aromas like these are the most common. The person you're reading will be very moved by these descriptions, so make sure that no matter how obscure the information seems, you convey it to them.

I've had many spirits play songs in my head during a reading. Because I grew up in my dad's dance studio, and I also competed in rollerskating, I have a pretty large musical dictionary in my head. The communication of song is very special because it brings back memories, so brush up on music from different decades so that you can speak their language.

## Advanced mediumship advice

Here's some advice for people who want to advance their mediumship abilities beyond typical information. Firstly, try not to waiver from the information that you receive, it's vital to trust the source. For instance, in a reading that I conducted, the deceased kept saying 'John' and I had to trust the information even though it was very general.

The person I was reading said, "He had a close relative named Joe."

My response was, "I know the difference between Joe and John, and he's not saying Joe, it's John."

The deceased then held up his hands and touched all his fingertips together before drawing them apart, out to his sides.

This communicated to me that he was saying the name is longer than just John. I asked my sitter if Johnson was a family name. She said, "Yes, it's my mother's maiden name."

I said, "Well, your son is around the Johnson family members, including your mother."

My sitter was very touched, and she could feel content in knowing that her reading was not only emotionally fulfilling but solid information.

Playing charades with the Otherside can sometimes be puzzling, but if you follow their lead and you have enough life experience, you can decode their messages. Stick with what they tell you, and trust your instincts; you can't let your sitter steer a reading, they can offer input, but ultimately you have to let the deceased guide you in order to conduct a sincere and accurate reading.

If you receive a piece of information that seems strange, share it anyway because those details are often important to the living. The deceased have fond memories of their lives, and the people they've loved for so long, and they take it all with them. Sometimes being an interpreter to the dead makes you a part of some personal information, very personal. Be prepared! I've brought through husbands who comment on their wife's figure in an attempt to flirt with them.

I love it when I get a spirit with a sense of humor, who jokes around with the person I'm reading. It's actually quite common, because fortunately many people are very funny. I like the men from the 1950s and 1960s who enjoy tossing a few back and tell their buddies their dirtiest joke. I've brought through some saucy gals, as well. Basically, some people revel in life, and there are others, unfortunately, who do not.

Learning how to interpret how someone felt when they died can be physically taxing on you, but being good at it is important if you want to be an exceptional medium who changes lives for the better. There are a lot of variables in readings and the more you read people the stronger you'll get. If you feel nauseous, that's usually the sensation they had around the time of their death. Usually nausea is because they had medication in their system making them sick, or sometimes it's because they had stomach cancer. Pain in your chest means 'trauma to the chest'; that's usually a heart attack, or a steering wheel hitting their chest in a car accident, but it's not limited to these. If you feel pain in your head during a reading, that's 'trauma to the head'; this can be from a gunshot wound to the head, car accident, occasionally an aneurysm, or because the person fell and hit their head around their time of death. However, if all you get is their head being 'highlighted' as a source of pain around their time of death, then just say that. Your sitter will know the cause, you can just convey the source of pain for the deceased.

Often, people who die from cancer will talk about their hair being beautiful again or like it was when they were healthy. For me, the deceased regularly highlight the chest area, with no thump to my chest, so that I know it wasn't a heart attack; this tells me it's very likely that they had emphysema or cancer in their chest. There are a lot of ways to die, so learning to read their feeling at the 'time of death' is extremely vital to a solid reading.

Take your time when interpreting the information. When I do an hour-long reading, I will bring through multiple people. However, if a half-hour is booked, I usually limit it to bringing through one person; unless the sitter wants to talk to their parents and then I assign fifteen minutes to each parent.

When you finish a reading, make sure that you disconnect from the people whom you brought through, so they don't stick around. When you wrap up your reading, you can use my conclusion and say, 'I'm going to break my connection with your (mom, dad, etc.) and I'm going to send them with you.'

## ADVICE FROM A PRACTICING MEDIUM

When a novice medium begins to sort out their feelings about their gift, it can be confusing. I hope this chapter helps people to understand that talking to the deceased is a gift, not a curse. Throughout the writing of this book, I asked a fellow medium to share her advice for people with mediumship abilities who are trying to understand the information they receive. I think it helps to have a couple of perspectives, so here's what my friend Tania has to say. Tania, is a professional medium, who has a light hearted flair and reads with empathy. I met her while on tour in Canada several years ago and she has become a trusted friend.

### LEARN TO TRUST YOUR OWN STYLE — BY TANIA THOMAS

I have watched many young or fledgling mediums eager to share their gifts make one very common mistake: Emulating the delivery or style of the older or more seasoned intuitive.

The best advice that I can offer is that you find your own unique way to deliver the message while maintaining the validity of the same. Never think for a moment that spirit is going to work with you in the same manner that they work with everyone else. The color blue may mean something different for another person to what it would mean to you. So, in a nutshell, stay with your own authentic style.

Learn the art of trust.

Early on I learned that those on the Otherside would use specific cues to provide me with the direction we needed to be going. One example is when someone sits with me that has lost a child and I will hear the song 'Somewhere Over the Rainbow' come into my mind. Alternatively, the old commercial jingle 'Gonna Wash that Man Right out of My Hair' indicates a relationship issue that appears to have no resolve.

Certain colors or smells will also be very indicative of the direction of the reading. Purple tells me that the sitter is intuitive in their own right. It may not mean the same thing for you, so it is imperative to trust what your own guides are providing you in terms of your own practice. Discover early into your path how they choose to work with you. Pay attention when you are around people and you will quickly understand that 'feeling sick to my stomach' may actually indicate someone you wish to stay clear of rather than a physical stomach issue.

Ask the spirit to assist you in understanding sides of the family. The easiest way to do this is to ask them to bring your own parents' energy, or your grandparents' energy, and 'place it' around you. Do you feel Mom's energy to your right or to your left? Note any tingling sensations, warmth or coolness to ascertain the direction in which they are coming from. I know immediately if a grandparent is maternal or paternal just by where they position themselves, either next to a female figure or a male figure. You'll get a distinct feeling that you're picking up on either feminine or masculine energy connected to the deceased, and that tells you which side of the family they're related to. In order to be able to receive information from the Otherside, I have to allow the deceased to work with me, through me, and I have to trust that they are there for the greater good of the living. Once you learn this, you will always be able to say with absolute certainty that I have your grandmother on mother's side standing with you. And you will be correct!

I use touch and smell in order to determine different sensations in a reading. When I smell a floral scent, I know that I'm dealing with a woman who either wore floral perfume or liked flowers. It's usually their perfume that I'm smelling. If a spirit is present and the aroma comes around me, I know right away that I am dealing with someone very loving, open and inviting. The key here is to practice—a lot!

The sense of 'touch' usually has more to do with them touching us. If the deceased was numb when they died, I'll feel numb myself, because they're touching me and conveying that sensation. Numbness to me usually means that there was medication in their system at the time of death, but not always. If the numbness is from the loss of a lot of blood, I'll see the color red and that tells me a different story.

Trust your information, own it. Never try to put a spin on what you are seeing, hearing or feeling. We're playing charades with the Otherside, the sitter will know why the information was important to the deceased loved one.

If you are ever overwhelmed with a sense of pressure in the

chest area, then say, 'I have pressure in the chest area.' If you are overwhelmed with a sense of dizziness, then express that feeling. You might say that this 'may' be indicative of a heart issue or a stroke, but never assume that you are correct. There are many ways to die. Receive all of the tidbits of information and you'll be able to form a more complete picture. I have learned that dizzy may actually indicate emotionally spinning out of control and this might correlate to a severe emotional disturbance leading to suicide, or even a car that is rolling following an accident. Don't be too quick to make an assumption, but interpret your information the best that you can.

## TRUSTING FIRST INSTINCTS

Joe and I also have 'family game night' with the girls, and we see it as a valuable tool to teach them how to trust their first instincts. For example, we play a game called 'Loaded Questions' (a card game sold in toy stores). The point of the game is to know by how the players answered a question, who it was that contributed each answer to your question. We were able to show the girls that whenever they second-guessed themselves, they lost points. When they trusted their gut-instinct, they gained points. So we practiced until they became comfortable trusting their first instincts.

If you think about it, we have to be programmed to trust and rely on ourselves. You'd think that would come naturally, but we've become comfortable relying on another person's opinion or insight, rather than our own. I guess it's sort of the 'grass is always greener on the other side of the fence' scenario.

Trusting your first instinct does actually have to be self-taught because, unfortunately, as we get older, our head gets filled with alternative opinions, and critical thinking becomes our new method. Over-analysis seems to be second nature to all of us 'type A' personalities, as well as a character trait of those who doubt themselves.

Those who trust their first instincts will save themselves a world of hurt. People avoid dangerous situations every day by trusting their first instinct. I encourage all sensitives to practice and strengthen their skills, no matter what their age is. Some people have a little bit of the gift and they should use it in their daily life. Others are working on mastering enormous abilities that will become their life and sometimes a profession. Either way, foster your gift, celebrate it being a part of you–you're one of the lucky ones. I'd rather feel too much, than not at all.

## Tips for Parents with Gifted Children

Sometimes I forget how unsettling seeing spirits can be for kids. On occasion I will watch a movie like *The Sixth Sense*, and I'm reminded how confusing it can be for children learning to communicate with spirits.

When I was a little girl, I never felt alone because spirits were always there protecting me, they were my friends, and sometimes roommates, who would eventually just go away. It didn't seem strange to me because it's all I knew. From the deceased's perspective they were just drawn to a little red-headed girl who laughed a lot and had a strong spirit. I reminded them of their daughters, nieces, sisters and sometimes of themselves, so they watched me play games and dress my dolls. I would watch the old men play checkers, and they would tell me 'stories'. I didn't realize that they weren't exactly there in body, that the stories they were telling me were of their living loved ones, who they still visited to share in their lives. They were describing the grandkids who could see them, and knew they were around, and how I reminded them of their granddaughters. It didn't strike me as odd that they were in my room, the conversations felt natural, and they felt 'safe' to me.

In childhood I was fine with spirits, but in my teens I started to feel weird because my friends would chalk up what I'd say to, 'It's just Allison'. Then my predictions became a little darker because my energy was changing as I grew, I was being prepped by the Otherside to deal with death and all that comes with it. I started being able to identify the sensation for 'cheating' or 'violence'. My friends would ask me what I thought of their boyfriend, and I could see exactly how the relationship would unfold. When I was eighteen I went to a funeral for a friend, and I saw him standing next to his casket. Life began to get very complicated for me as I became a young adult, and then I met Joe, my stabilizing force!

I weathered my youth pretty well for a kid with a mysterious gift. Not all kids are as lucky as I was, some 'feel' too much and they can't handle the overwhelming visions and sensations. Sometimes having a gift—whether it's the ability to communicate with the dead, a beautiful voice or athletic prowess—can be the very thing that takes away your sense of self. So finding a balance in life is crucial for everyone, you can never let one thing define who you are, you need to develop all aspects of you.

Some of my best tips for parents with gifted children are quite simple. Letting your child know that they can tell you anything is key to getting them to be comfortable with their gift and open up to you. Remember, kids can feel it if you don't believe them, so being sincerely supportive is necessary.

For parents without abilities, be prepared to hear things that may seem 'out there' to you. Your child might see angels that they will describe as tall and sombre-looking. Angels have very positive energy, but they're also warriors, so they can appear to be intimidating in size and demeanor. They act as protection, especially for children. I've seen angels a few times and they're very powerful to look at, the ones that I see around me are sometimes enormous in height, and I don't worry about anything when they're around because I know that nothing bad can get to me, because the bad would have to get passed them, and that's not happening. So if your child sees angels, it's a good thing because it means that your child is under their protection.

Another strange sighting can be what I call 'mischievous' energy, and as far as I can tell, they were living pranksters that still like stirring up trouble. I saw one of these once. It was a cloudy white color and would wrap its head around the corner and peek at me, but then faster than humanly possible it would pull its head back, so I couldn't see it anymore. It just kept repeating this over and over. My mantra to deal with these entities involves asking the Otherside to 'block any negative or mischievous entities from me and my family, not allowing them to be around us or come in contact with us'. This has always worked for me, and I highly recommend it.

A child is never too young to experience something supernatural. My kids were toddlers when they started telling Joe and I that they were seeing spirits. Kids at that age are hesitant to tell people what they observed, because they're not really sure what they're seeing, so it's hard for them to articulate. So, if you have a really young child telling you that they see an apparition in their room, believe them and be supportive.

Children are very appealing to spirits, because they are the brightest of energies, and the deceased love to be around them. Especially infants; they like to make funny faces at and make them laugh. I think babies are the closest in energy to spirits because they have no chip on their shoulder or issues. Once a child is old enough to draw, you can ask them to draw a picture of the spirit they see, and the images that the spirit shows your child. It's like kindergarten automatic writing with crayons—I love it!

As gifted children get older, let them practice on you, pull impressions off you. This is okay as long as their family and friends are open to spiritual connections. I tell our kids not to talk about what we do at school because not everybody can see what we see. For little kids, just tell them they have 'special eyes' that see what some people can't. Most importantly, let them know that what they can do is a good thing; it's not bad or strange, but very normal amongst feeling beings. Animals can sense the Otherside because they use their instincts all the time, so sensing spirits is second nature to them. Kids also have heightened energy because they are emotionally based, like spirits. As they get older, it's necessary to make sure that they continue to trust their instincts. One day it may save their life.

An exercise that I do with our kids is to give them each a pad of paper then I tell them the name of a relative who died long ago and they write it down. I let them practice pulling impressions off the name that I gave them at the top of their pad of paper , I encourage them to do their best and write down anything that they hear or that comes to mind. Afterwards, I let them know how proud I am of them, both for their openness to try automatic writing and for the information that they were willing to trust. Sometimes you have to fact-check their information with an older generation, and sometimes you won't be able to verify what they got, but that doesn't mean they're wrong, either. Sometimes the details will seem obscure, but often those are the most special pieces to the puzzle. When treated as a game, it's actually fun to do. Our kids are always amazed at how accurate and straightforward their information is. So am I, and I'm a proud Mama Bear, too.

The information they get should be mostly positive, and if their information is mostly dark and negative, then you have to look at other possibilities rather than psychic/mediumship tendencies. A child's personality is going to factor into how they process the information they receive, as well as how they interact with spirits. This is the same for adult mediums, too. If you have a funny, light-hearted child, they will pull positive, fun family members from the Otherside. Even the deceased who were grumpy in life are able to share their lighter energy with an upbeat kid.

A child who has temper issues or acts out negatively regularly will draw dark energy to them, because like attracts like. In essence, they speak the same language. So kids who talk about mostly the dark stuff may have some underlying personal problems that are going to be made worse by their gift acting as a portal to negative entities. Addressing behavioral problems or depression in a child will help them to hopefully heal and shift their energy, which will give them focus, allowing their abilities to act as a gift—not a curse. The healthier and happier the child, the greater their potential will be to become a phenomenal psychic/medium in adulthood.

Parents, when you're working with your kids, keep in mind that by you being open to their abilities, you will begin to see more of your own. So play the games with them, and work on not dismissing it when you're right about an impression, or more likely that you'll 'get' the same impression as your child at exactly the same time.

With little girls, or even little boys, you can use something as simple as a doll to teach them. Tell your child to close their eyes. Then pick an outfit for the doll and hide it behind your back. Tell them to visualize what color outfit you chose. If it's too hard for them, just have them tell you if the color feels warm or cold. This can help them learn red (warm) or blue (cold). This game really does help them determine colors, and that is very important in readings. It's how we know the color of the deceased's clothing, their hair color, etc. They don't always show us their image; sometimes they have to convey color through feeling. For me, black comes through as a 'hard' feeling, like a tarred road; white comes through as a 'soft' feeling, like a cloud. Sometimes children are just really good at this 'game' and can just see the colors, straight up!

Keep in mind that everyone has their own style, but that's how it works for me. It's also fun to play this game with food. If they can tell you the color of the treat that's covered in the bowl, they can have it. Use several treats, because we don't want any children going hungry! It can be as simple as a grape or a strawberry for this game, it doesn't have to be anything particularly special in order to teach them.

Helping your kids to realize their talents is one of the most loving gestures that you can make as a parent. Love your children unconditionally, and tell them often that they are special and you're so glad that they are yours.

### E<small>NJOY YOUR READING</small>

I particularly enjoy readings that start out teary and end with my sitter laughing at what their deceased loved one is saying to them through me. Readings seem to make people nervous as their anticipation paired with their desire to connect builds. So I usually spend the first few minutes of a reading trying to get the sitter to relax, so they're in a good place to hear the messages that I have for them. I always advise my audiences to only raise their hand for a reading if they *feel* ready, otherwise they won't be in a place to hear the messages or receive the calm that a reading can bring to their soul.

I had a reading with a woman named Sue; she was anxious to hear from her friend Pamela, as she missed her terribly. Pamela wasn't hard to bring through, she had young energy even though she wasn't young when she passed away. Pamela wanted Sue to visualize her at 27, since that's the age she chose to revert to after she died. Later in the reading Sue realized that she herself had been 27 when she met Pamela, so she thought that was funny. Pamela thanked Sue for the 'photographs' and told her she loved them; as it turned out, Sue is a photographer and she had taken some professional pictures of Pamela's family before Pam died.

Pam wanted to talk about the 'big birthday', and that means a milestone birthday, usually one that ends in a zero. She said that she was there for it. Sue explained to me that she and a friend had traveled to my Seattle event to celebrate their 40th and 50th birthdays. So as they sat in the ballroom with me, Pamela was there with them. Sue told me later that I had given her friend a life reading at my event, one that helped her on to a new professional path, a path that created a space for her to feel good again. I never get tired of hearing good things about the people I've read, and some people actually take my advice!

During the reading with Sue, I asked, "Did Pam use to have red in her hair?"

Sue responded, "Yes, she did!"

So I was seeing the right person. I then understood very clearly what Pam was doing; she was trying to remove the memory of her being sick and older, so that Sue could feel at ease that Pam was youthful and full of life again. This is a common practice of the deceased; they're attempting to adjust our energy, aka soul, so that we lighten up and walk with a bounce in our step again. We tend to get stuck trying to empathize with the deceased in their last moments of life and we become unable to move forward with them because we've taken on so much pain.

Once they adjust our energy, we can move forward with them, and they can now access us in dreams and in life, and share their wisdom of living with us all.

At one point Sue said, "Ask her who's going to help me paint and decorate now. I don't know what color to paint my wall."

Pamela replied, "Lavender."

Sue paused and then started laughing. "She would pick a shade of purple!" She explained that their taste in colors differed, but the point of the message was that Pam was still ready to help her friend.

Pam went on to say that she liked the casino, and Sue shared that they worked together in a shop in a casino and those are some of her fondest memories.

There were a lot of messages that were special, but I shared this reading because it made me feel good to take part in their 'hen party' that day. I share examples of readings to try to remove the fear or hesitation that people have about communicating with deceased loved ones. A reading should be a positive experience, and, if it's not, you need to find a new medium. You need a medium who will fit your personality, just remember not to use them as a crutch. An annual reading can be fine, but you don't want to be read too often or the messages and feeling of the reading will weaken.

The deceased are interactive in readings, it's not just mediums passing on their messages. A reading lets you know the deceased on a personal level, who they are, and what their life made them feel like. A reading provides jigsaw puzzle pieces, fragments of the deceased's life that when connected together shows you a complete picture of a unique life.

## THE DECEASED'S PERSPECTIVE

The way the deceased see our readings is just as a way to reach us so that we know they're all right, a way to help us to connect with them ourselves, and to assist us in rejoining the living to finish our own story. Pam was reaching out to Sue for those reasons, she saw it as an opportunity to visit her friend, and a way to remove any guilt that her friend might have felt about not being able to be there when she passed away. Pam's agenda was to breathe life into her friend, and to let her know that she was not alone. Pam came through with the smallest details—the cornerstones of who she is—she knew what Sue needed to hear, and she made it happen.

## BE OPEN TO THE MESSAGE

When I started my reading with Brenda, I was struck by a giant wall of pain constructed the moment that she lost her daughter. I always feel very deeply for parents who lose their children, no matter the child's age at the time of their passing. I can't think of anything more unbearable.

Brenda's daughter, who I'll call 'Emily', came through rather easily, and she showed herself with a cat on her lap. Now that might seem basic, and some mediums might even be hesitant to mention the cat without getting a name, but the cat proved to matter very much to Brenda since her daughter had left her favorite cat to her. Emily said that she was 'numb, cold and couldn't feel much at the time that she died, but she felt confused'.

As a medium, I've learned to interpret this description as medication being in the system of the dying.

Emily said that she reverted to being sixteen, because that was the age that she was able to be with her mother still, and she felt free, full of life. She talked about being around her brother. She mentioned that January was important to her; when I'm told a month, I know it is either the birth month or month of passing. January was, in fact, Emily's birthday month.

She relayed many beautiful messages and showed objects connected to her, but one thing that moved Brenda is when Emily said, 'I want to watch *Steel Magnolias* with you, Mom.' Brenda said that was her daughter's favorite movie, and now she knows that she can still have movie nights with her.

The reason that I'm sharing this reading is because, not only is it profound, but it's a good learning tool for mediums. Emily kept saying to me that she tried to reach her mother through her friend 'Julie'. Brenda didn't know what that meant, but she thought that maybe I meant 'Judy'; that worried me because I don't negotiate my information with my sitter. Yet I also have to stay open to the chance that maybe I'm misinterpreting my information. Misinterpreting names for me only happens if the name is highly unusual, something I've never heard before, and then I can only get a name that sounds the closest to the unusual name, it has to be something that I'm familiar with. 'Julie' is my first cousin's name so, I'm very familiar with the name, so I had no doubt in this case but I just moved on. It's best to keep the momentum of a reading going, even if your client hasn't had the light bulb moment yet, where they get what the deceased is trying to get across to them.

At the end of the reading, Brenda expressed to me that she was sorry that I had moved one of my events on my tour, because her daughter's friend Julie had wanted to get her tickets and bring her to my event. There it was—'Julie'. Emily had tried to work through her friend to reach her mother, so that she could speak to her through me, just like she had said earlier in the reading.

It's common in readings that the sitter is a little stunned, because it's highly emotional to reconnect with someone who you miss so much. Readings will elevate emotions, and processing the information given by the medium can be difficult, when emotionally the sitter is in overdrive. When I begin a reading, I always tell my sitter that there may be a piece of information they can't make sense of at the time, but that it still means something important, otherwise the deceased wouldn't mention it, and so the sitter should just think about it later. Trust your information, and recognize that your sitter is just absorbing so much emotional information that it's occasionally too much for them to process. I look forward to meeting Brenda and Julie in person at my event, since Emily spent so much energy on making the reading happen.

### The Deceased's Perspective

Emily was pulling out all the stops to make sure that her mother got what she needed. The deceased can feel frustrated at times, but it just fuels them to try even harder to get through to their loved ones. The deceased are pulling all of the strings when it comes to the living. They are powerful, and lively, they have endless amounts of energy to give to us. Emily was not going to give up on her mother, just like her mother never gave up on her. When you're telling your deceased loved one what you really need from them, be certain that they will find a way to give it to you, but you have to be open to them, otherwise you're inaccessible. When you're inaccessible, you won't see their signs and/or you'll dismiss their messages as wishful thinking. Even so, they remain determined to find people willing to hear them, to pass on their messages to you; it's up to you whether or not you want to listen.

## Cyber readings

I never thought that social media would provide a way for spirits to reconnect with their loved ones, but I guess it shouldn't be a surprise, since both consist of electric energy. I had a Facebook friend named Cheryl who had recently lost her son Danny in a car accident. I know that I'm just one person so I can't read everyone but her loss weighed on me during the holidays. So on December 30th I messaged her and asked if she was available because I wanted to read her; she was, and I did. I know that when I'm moved to read a person at a particular time, it's because the Otherside is doing it for a reason. It turned out that the prior New Year's Eve, Cheryl's son had rushed home to give her a hug. So through the reading he was trying to ease her anxiety for the following night, because as Cheryl shared with me, she missed her son, and she had been dreading New Year's Eve festivities without him.

## THE DECEASED'S PERSPECTIVE

Danny knew that his mom was struggling, and when people are grieving they often take antidepressants or anti-anxiety medication. Medication can make it harder for the living to 'feel' the deceased around them, so another avenue must be taken by spirits to reach the living. Danny seemed to feel that I was the right way to connect with his mother, and he succeeded in bringing me to her.

It was hard for Danny to watch his mother suffer, needing to hold him, wanting him back again. He saw her struggle with sleeping, and he witnessed the rippling effect that his death had on the people who loved him. A rippling effect that swelled into a tidal wave of pain that threatened to drown out any happiness his loved ones might experience in his absence.

Once Danny had the opportunity to be heard by his mom, his messages came pouring out, as he walked her through some of the greatest days of his life. His purpose in reminiscing with her was to show her how lucky he had been in his life, and how loved he felt. He told her that he relived his brightest moments constantly, and he didn't feel loss because his mom was still vacationing on the beach with him. She was still watching his sports teams on television with him, and cheering them on! She was still a part of his daily life. Danny's love grew as he spoke and shared what he saw with his mother, as well as his excitement to talk to her and be heard, which was all he had wanted. Danny said, 'I don't want my life to be reduced to death.'

Danny wanted his mom to add hang-gliding to her bucket list, since he hadn't gotten around to it. He was attempting to resuscitate her life, jumpstart her soul back to living again. He lived in the physical world for only nineteen years, but he'll never grow old and he'll still be able to sample life through the people who love him.

It's important for mediums to remember that if you're supposed to read someone, the deceased will bring you together, sometimes even through social media; whatever and however they can, they'll make it happen. Don't approach people you don't know and ambush-read them—as I've said, it's unethical, and we have no right. Remember that it's about the wounded, not about us. If people aren't being sent your way for readings by the universe, it may not be your calling, and that's okay. Many mediums try and force a professional career, but just because you can communicate with spirits, that doesn't mean it's going to be your 'job'. Just do what you can when the universe sends you a clear signal that this is a person you can help.

## My events

My events are necessary since they allow me to touch more people at once, rather than long, individual scheduled readings. This is why I limit the size of my audience, it's more intimate, I want to be able to connect with my whole audience. I don't want my events to be a show but rather a deep experience.

The energy at my events varies depending on the trauma of the city, or the people at my events who are a microcosm of the city. Occasionally, and thankfully, sometimes I'll have an event that has no 'murder' readings—this happens in Australia but in the United States it's unfortunately common. These events are quite traumatic for not only the personally affected family and friends of the deceased, but my audience is impacted as well, as they empathize with the victim. Murders, suicides and loss of children are the heaviest themes that I see run through my events, and the living who are left behind to pick up the pieces are devastated. Sometimes I'll even get a murder/suicide and that messes with my head a little because I'm used to enjoying connecting with the deceased, but when the deceased killed another, I find myself repelled and saddened.

Even though the readings can weigh on me, there are light moments that stand out for me, too. I recently read a very nice man whose deceased brother kept talking about having a mustache, then the man happily reached into his bag and pulled out a big photo of his brother with a very handsome, profound mustache. He shared it with my audience and they enjoyed being able to look at the photo shown by the now proud man, who missed the connection that had been lost when his brother killed himself. The energy of the suicide created a constant vacuum of pain for the living brother. Through the joy of sharing the picture of his brother with the audience and the affection coming from my audience to him, he was able to smile. He had begun the process of remembering the good times, by doing this, he allowed his brother to come back in to his life. The reconnection had been made and they were now on the same energy page, once again wanting to be in one another's lives.

At the same event I had a lovely young man who had died far too soon come through and he talked about many aspects of his life, including the love of his family, but when he shared that 'My

Way' was the right song to play at his memorial, his family was floored. That was his favorite Frank Sinatra song. They had, indeed, played it for him—and now he was able to tell them he heard and loved it. You'd think that because the deceased was so young that he would have gravitated to a song more current, but he related to the crooners who were singing many decades before he was even born he was an old soul, he liked, what he liked!

At another event I read a woman who had lost her sister, and the woman that I was reading was a bit 'in her head', pragmatic, I guess, so I think that her deceased sister wanted to really drive it home that she was there. So the deceased sister told me her name, 'Ann', and that's all it took; we all watched the woman's emotional wall crumble. Ann wasn't just the deceased sister's name, it was also the woman's daughter's middle name. So with the simple message, Ann did two things; she convinced her sister that she was there in the room with us, while acknowledging her name connection to her niece, who she still loves and dotes on.

Events always have upsides. My audience learns from me and they get a sense of peace from their deceased loved ones, and I learn from the deceased. I also get to meet an array of people, both living and dead. When the energy is right at one of my events, there's a lot of laughter, tears and bonding between myself, my audience and the Otherside.

### The deceased's perspective

The deceased really run the show at my events, and the strongest energies will push through to be heard. The people who lived a long life often step aside, so the younger people can be heard in an effort to reduce their family's trauma. Young males, teenage through to early 20-somethings, tend to be not good at waiting their turn to be heard, and they will take over another person's reading if the other energy is weaker than they are; it all rides on who has the most energy to come through. Little kids are extremely easy to bring through and, being a mom, I really do enjoy them, and I can empathize with their parents' pain. Children, in my opinion, are the easiest of all to bring through.

## How do you know a psychic or medium is reliable?

It's important for people who are looking for a spiritual advisor to know what to look for, because as with any profession, there are people in it for the right reasons, and some are in it for purely selfish ones. I believe that personal recommendations are really the safest way to find a psychic/medium. Some mediums get 'certification', but what does that really mean? If a spiritual advisor is truly great at their craft, then word-of-mouth will keep them booked solid for at least a few months. So I personally don't find certification to be a sure-fire way to find someone legitimate in my field. It doesn't mean they're no good, it just isn't a guarantee that your reading will be amazing.

One of the warning signs you should look out for is if the person you go to says something like, 'You have a bad energy around you, and if you pay me X amount of dollars, I'll remove it from your aura.' Some unethical practitioners use scare tactics and tell you that 'you'll never find love' or 'you'll never be happy' unless you pay them to remove the spell or bad energy in your life. If they say anything similar to this, simply walk out!

Also, don't use a psychic/medium as a permanent crutch; one great mediumship reading should be enough. Sometimes people want to have a reading annually, and that's okay, but I won't do it weekly or monthly. Also, if you go to multiple mediums, the deceased person you want to contact will lose energy on coming through, because they've already conveyed their messages. So be careful not to overdo the mediumship readings; they're intimate, special experiences. Psychic readings can be done a little more frequently, but I always believe that your inner voice will do most of the guiding in your life. If you want guidance, look within. And if you need an advisor, make sure they have an accurate track record.

An ethical medium would never give a mediumship reading that leaves their sitter feeling worse at the end, or say something like, 'Well, they tried to come through but "so and so" wouldn't listen.' If the deceased wants to come through to the living, they will find a way to, not blame others for not listening, so that's nothing a legitimate medium would ever say came from the deceased. A medium I saw on television blamed another for not relaying a message to the living from the deceased. News flash! You're a medium, how about you pass on the message from the deceased, instead of pointing fingers. Spirits, *don't* blame people for not listening to them, they understand there are various reasons why, the timing may not be right for the living.

I've also heard from parents who've lost children that a medium has told them that their child is 'stuck'. In all of my experience reading more than 10,000 people, I've never seen a child 'stuck' between worlds. Children always have multiple people waiting for them. Young people have no problem transitioning between worlds, they may choose to still hang out at home with their family but they're not bound here. They stay by choice.

An ethical medium handles their clients with empathy and understanding. A great medium will be able to deliver a solid reading in the tone and personality of the deceased, and their sense of humor remains intact, as well as sarcasm or any outstanding personality traits.

## PROFESSIONAL MEDIUMS

The intention for any medium to provide readings should always be to give an emotional boost to their client, helping them to move forward. A person who is a medium may not have the personality to do it professionally, there is a degree of charisma involved. A great medium can align their energy with their client's most of the time. Some mediums don't have the ability to adjust their energy in order to align and access the client emotionally.

Obviously, a medium's personality will set the tone for the reading, so it's a huge factor in being able to be a medium professionally. Occasionally, a medium and a client won't vibe— I mean, we're all human! If you're having trouble making a connection with the person you're reading and you're ten minutes into the session, stop the reading and suggest they try a medium that they click with for the best possible result. Don't try and 'prove yourself', you'll end up wasting an hour just to hear that you basically gave a lukewarm reading. Then, you're not happy and they're not happy. Cut your losses early on and chalk it up to 'not meant to be'. Our intention is for the grieving to have the reading that they need and if it's not with you, that's okay!

Always do the 'work' because it helps others; if you always have the right intention and precise boundaries, you'll be fine, no matter what level your gift takes you to in life.

# Premature death

If you've been to my events, then you know that I explain to my audience that I don't bring through children under two-years of age at my events. The reason for this is because children under two don't have a lot of life experience, and their vocabulary is very limited. They can come through, but only briefly and most of the reading sounds general, because they were so young. For instance, they had a favorite stuffed animal, they liked cereal, they liked to play in the bath tub, etc. So that's why I don't do it at events.

Being a mother of three girls, though, I do understand how the love of a child feels, and the thought of losing something so precious is unimaginable. When I was seven months pregnant with our daughter Fallon, I was told she may not make it, and to prepare myself for the worst. While I was pregnant, I had bought a baby outfit for her to wear the day that she was born. I didn't know if she would be alive, but I knew that I loved her. I'll never shake the fear I felt when I thought that I could lose her, and I'll never forget the relief I felt when she was born healthy. Fortunately for us, she not only made it to full term, she was our biggest baby, who shoved peas in her mouth at three months of age, to show me that her 17-pound body needed more than other babies her age.

I wrote this chapter for parents who have lost very young children or babies who never even took a breath. I think they need to be remembered, too.

## Baby angels

When babies don't make it through the pregnancy, whether from a natural occurrence, an accident or even a termination, the soul of the child usually recycles back into your family. What I mean by that is, it could be that a baby you have in the family somewhere down the line could carry the soul. A niece or nephew of yours, a future grandchild of yours, someone born later in the family, is a portal for the soul of the baby you lost. For whatever reason the timing wasn't right, your baby wasn't able to come into the world in a body that wasn't healthy enough to sustain a full life, Or, under the circumstances of the parents, sometimes the mother isn't physically strong enough to carry to term, that doesn't mean the baby won't find a way to be a part of your family.

It's not fair, and it doesn't even seem natural, that a baby would be born deceased, it's hard to fathom. My mom gave birth to a son that was no longer alive due to a car accident, so I had another brother. When I was small, I use to ask her if I had another brother, I just felt like I did, and it turned out he was real. If he had lived, I wouldn't be here; I think I was intended to fill that void, and that's okay. We don't always know why bad things happen, and I hope that my brother found his way into the family. Apparently, it was my time to be born, and I'm glad that by writing this chapter I can honor a brother that no one ever talked about. I see how much it still affects my mom, and I know that she and my brother will always have a special bond.

## YOUNG SPIRITS

I find nothing as hard to understand as young people dying. When you have a baby, you just assume that they'll have a long life, and then you watch them grow into beautiful people with stars in their eyes. When that light is extinguished, it diminishes our own light as we struggle to come to terms with losing them. I take bringing children through very personally, having three daughters of my own.

I'm an advocate for spirits and the living as well, I try to energetically align the world of the living with the existence of the dead. Young spirits make this very easy for me because they have such a bright light about them and they usually really like to talk. It's rare that I get a young person with low energy, they are almost always vibrant, and they know how to project their energy. They are delightful, and they want their families to know that they are still a part of the family portrait.

I brought through a very special girl named Simone for her sister Hayley, and later unbeknown to me, for her mother. When I conduct a reading, I go off the first name of the sitter and the first name of the deceased; that's all. Once I've established young energy as being the deceased, I usually get a knot in my stomach because I know the reading is going to be very painful for my sitter. Simone came through easily, eager to talk to her sister. The messages came fast, and clear, she didn't want to talk about how she died but she was keen to talk about everything else. I don't think that she wanted to waste time talking about her death, but rather spend our half-hour speaking to her family, knowing what they needed.

I have to add that, out of the tens of thousands of readings I've done, Simone was the first to mention liking Justin Beiber. I found this funny since I had to listen to hours of his music with my daughter, talk about parent torture! but since he was her favorite I guess I can understand. Hayley had a good laugh about it, and it's the laughter in a reading that raises the energy and makes the reconnection complete. Laughter is spontaneous, and it shows that the sitter's heart and soul has accepted that this is their loved one who they're talking to. Hayley was accepting Simone's presence and it was beautiful.

### A SISTER'S LOVE – HAYLEY'S STORY

I grew up in a small country town of Victoria, Australia, with my parents, my brother Brad, who is two and a half years younger than me, and my sister Simone, who came quite a bit later, more than seven years after me, in May 1994.

I still remember this day as a seven-year-old very clearly, as I was at home with mom when she went into strong labour—with nobody else in sight, no mobile phones, and Dad out on the farm, it was a little scary for someone my age! All went well, though, and Dad came home in time to take mom to the hospital then, soon after, welcome the arrival of Simone Tori Mitchell. She was the sister I had wished upon every star for, since I had heard mom tell a friend over the phone that she was pregnant.

Growing up, I was a typical older sister, especially in my teenage years, and found my kid sister to be at times a little trying, but this was largely due to teenage intolerance, rather than anything else, as she was the most placid, easy-going child you would meet. It was later on, once I was older and she was around the age of fifteen and onwards, that the age gap seemed to become irrelevant, and we became closer and closer. Perhaps fortuitously, my mom, who was the eldest and had three brothers, used to say for as long as I remember, with great earnest, 'You are just so lucky to have a sister, I always wished I had a sister.' In those later years Simone and I would often say how lucky we were to have each other, as there really is nothing quite as special as the love and bond with a sister, especially when you're so lucky to have one like Simone.

In October 2012, Simone was studying hard for school exams. She visited my house often in between going to and from school and home to our parents. One weekend mom and Dad went away for a few nights, which rarely happened, for a family wedding. Simone and I organized for her to have dinner with me, my boyfriend (now my husband) and some friends at our favorite local cafe. I remember the last time I spoke to her on the phone, giggling and saying how we were both so glad she was coming —everything was always exciting, or hilarious, with Simone.

Devastatingly, she never arrived. When she did not appear at our house, my boyfriend and I drove out searching for her, and found her car had veered off the road, not far from our parents' house. She had been killed instantly. This was October 12, 2012. She was eighteen years old.

The first time we met Allison was at a seminar in Melbourne in March 2013. We had been hanging out for this seminar after one of mom's very dear friends had suggested it to us and booked our tickets. mom, her friend Kyla, my grandmother and myself arrived at the seminar full of anticipation and hope, and I remember spending a great deal of time silently talking to Simone and asking her to do her best to come through that night, although reassuring her we understood if she couldn't manage it —as Simone hated pressure and what pressure this was!

The seminar blew our minds with Allison's accuracy—then, not only did we finally get chosen for a reading, but the unusual events leading up to our reading were amazing. The more mom and I felt desperate as time ticked away, the louder others around us got. All of a sudden, two women behind us wanted to see our photo of Simone, then, as Joe was picking the next reading, part of the audience started jumping up and down and pointing at us to receive a reading. Meanwhile, the lady next to my mom fidgeted and jigged around in her seat constantly. We later found out she was also a medium, and she said that Simone's energy was so strong she was finding it difficult to hold it away from her and not be overwhelmed by it. Then to really shock us into attention, the poor woman who had a reading prior to us to bring her daughter through proceeded to look more and more confused. We, on the other hand, got more and more gobsmacked, as Allison sat and talked in detail about Simone, her accident, her life, and my upcoming wedding. Simone was hijacking the other reading! When we finally got to our reading, it was one of the most amazing experiences of our lives and I could just hear, see and feel Simone laughing and talking, smiling upon us. Her essence was so palpable in the room that night, and her strength as she came through was seriously mind-blowing.

A year later, I received a phone call from Joe, Allison's husband, asking if I would like a phone reading, as mom and I had put ourselves on the waiting list at the seminar. We promptly organized a reading the following week, after Joe assured me that my mom would also receive a reading later in the month. This was important to me, as I know there is no greater loss than the loss of a child, and I had seen so much of my parents' tremendous pain in the last year. Nobody deserved to speak to Simone more than mom.

On the morning Allison rang, I was sitting quietly in my sister's room at my mom and dad's house. Allison's voice was instantly warming. Allison and Joe are amazing in their ability to be so personable, it is as if you have known them for years. They are so truly amazing.

Allison began by telling me Simone had presented herself as seventeen, as this was the year she was at her happiest. She explained this is often because they do not like the year that they passed, so this was the year she chose. Allison said that Simone was my guardian angel, and that she often whispered in my ear. She said she was really proud of me as I heard her and, unlike most others, I did not try to explain it away. I often felt Simone was communicating with me, letting me know she was there, and what her opinion was on things—just like we always did with each other—but you do wonder sometimes if this is wishful thinking or truly happening, so I was very relieved to hear this.

Allison passed on to me what Simone was saying about how much she liked the bracelets that people wore for her. I immediately knew what she was talking about, as she had mentioned this at the seminar also. At the end of 2012, friends of Simone's at her high school had worn light blue (her favorite color) arm bands with 'SIMMY' written on them in her memory. They were still faithfully worn by many—not all of whom we knew—and it was common for us to walk around the local towns and randomly see a flash of blue on a wrist in a grocery store, at a restaurant, at the movies, anywhere! There was something very comforting about this, and I would often say to mom that it was like Simone's secret little army out there, all wearing this bracelet to show they were part of this special group of people who loved Simone and were touched by her life. Allison said it was important to Simone that everybody knew how much she loved the bracelets, so after the reading I posted it on Facebook for her friends.

Simone then proceeded to talk about Dad. My dad had a particularly hard time recently with the passing of his last remaining family member, his sister. It was all a bit much and he was struggling. Allison said he had something wrong with his heart or his blood pressure and that Simone was worried about him. My sister pointed out that he didn't breathe properly and took a lot of shallow breaths. She wanted to take some of his pain away, but he wouldn't let her. She said that he needed to take care of himself because mom and I needed him. Simone was also very insistent that we tell Dad that she had his 'black dog'. Dad had a sheep dog, Tess, for years, and he loved her dearly. Simone wanted him to know that Tess was okay, and with her!

My dad has suffered from high blood pressure for years, and lately we had seen him not taking care of himself, working himself to the point of exhaustion in the hot sun a number of times. My dad is a very shy, quiet and skeptical man, but when I passed on Simone's message I could see how profoundly it affected him. There is no doubt in my mind our poor dad understood her message.

Allison also discussed our brother, Brad. She said Simone saw him on the computer a lot, that he looked at it too much. He was constantly laying in his room these days, watching movies on his laptop as a way to relax. She said he also was starting something that was a challenge for him and that she was very proud of him. When I explained he had just started a university degree, which was a huge deal for someone who left school early, Allison said she could see him graduating. She also said Simone really liked the photo of the two of them that he had on the background of his computer. I had noticed this photo many times when his computer was laying around the house.

In our initial conversation, when Joe had told me to consider what questions I had for Allison, I thought long and hard about what Simone would want me to do. So I asked if there was anything she would like me to pass on to her best friend Esther and her boyfriend Mitch.

Allison had already stated that Simone had mentioned her concerns about Mitch, that people thought he was feeling better than he was, but that every day he thought of Simone and was finding things really tough. Simone said that he would often talk to her, asking her questions, and that she heard him. She was also worried about his drinking. In the last twelve months we had noticed that Mitch had started to party a lot more, but had thought he had become more social due to circumstance, as being a quieter guy he had previously tended to be a little reluctant to go out and Simone had been his main social outlet. Simone said that Mitch also needed to be careful with cars. When I passed this on to Mitch, he was gobsmacked. He said that the reading was 100 per cent accurate for him and made perfect sense. He was so thankful to have had that message passed on.

Esther was Simone's best friend, and they spent countless hours together, talking, playing crazy games and, most of all, laughing. Boy, did they laugh! Everything was hilarious and they could often be seen lying on the floor in fits of giggles. When Simone got her license, it was another great source of excitement for them both. It meant there were countless opportunities for girls' road trips, even if that was only two minutes down the road!

Allison began by saying that Simone was showing her the fun they both had together in a car, with the wind in their hair; however, since Simone's passing Esther was holding back doing something in regards to this. Simone was very keen for Esther to get back to it.

I explained that Simone, being slightly older, had always said to Esther she would teach her how to drive before she got her license. After the accident, Esther had lost all confidence and desire to drive and had never gotten her license.

The next message that Simone had for her best friend made Allison a little unsure of the accuracy of what she was hearing for a moment. Rather cautiously, Allison ask if Simone liked Justin Beiber as she was showing him to her. Now this really sent me into fits of giggles, and Allison soon joined in when I replied that Simone looooved Justin Beiber. She was always saying how much she loved his music and, despite his critics, she was always adamant that we all should watch his movie and then we would surely understand him better and become converts. Allison said that Simone kept repeating how awesome Justin was, and that she wanted Esther to listen to his music or go to a concert so that she could join in! Talk about insistent! Simone was still busy trying to convince us all!

Allison also said Simone knew Esther often wore a shirt of hers to feel close to her. I already knew Esther had a shirt of Simone's and later, when I asked her about it, she said that she did still wear it occasionally. In fact, when I passed all of Simone's messages on to Esther, she, too, was blown away by the accuracy of many of the details of the reading, and was also very thankful to be able to have these messages given to her, through Allison, from her best friend that she missed so much.

After this particularly humorous message, Allison then gave me a name of one of Simone's friends at school. Allison asked if I knew who this was, as she felt I had been in contact with him. When I established I did indeed know this friend, she stated that Simone wanted him to know that there was a male with her who was very important to this friend. When I explained that this friend had lost his brother in an accident, when the brother was quite young, Allison confirmed this was him, a young boy, and that Simone really wanted her friend to know that his brother was with her and happy. When I passed this on to that friend, he was astounded at the accuracy and so deeply touched and appreciative for that small piece of information; it put his heart slightly at ease about his brother.

Allison also stated that Simone was surrounded by children and that when they passed they gravitated towards her. This was very significant to me and our family, as Simone had an affinity with children, they were always drawn to her. She had a never-ending source of patience, and a humorous, vivacious nature, and she would play with them for hours on end. As long as I can remember, Simone loved children, no matter what age she was at! And they just adored her. When she was growing up, Simone always said she was going to be a volunteer clown in the hospital to make little kids feel better. I am sure she would have achieved that goal, and been very good at it, indeed. mom always said Simone was born half clown!

Allison said my sister also wanted us to know she ate whatever she liked, including lots of ice cream. Simone was a very fit, slim athlete and excelled at all sports, but, boy, was her stomach a bottomless pit! She loved her food, and ice cream was one of the favorites. So I was very happy to hear this.

Simone also wanted us to know that she had missed out on nothing in life, that she was really happy, her life was a great life, full of love, and that she still continued to enjoy it. She felt she had the experience of being a mother because of all the children around her now, and she knew what it was like to love and be loved, because of her relationship with Mitch. She did, however, miss Mom playing with her hair. Mom was always doing amazing things with Simone's beautiful long thick blonde hair, so I was not surprised to hear this; they were extremely close. This bit of information really touched my heart and I know it also mattered greatly to my parents.

Allison said that Simone was trying to communicate through music, and that it was her way of letting us know she was still around. There had been a number of occasions when we would be out for a meal or ice cream—which Simone often did with us—and certain songs she loved would come on, in different versions, some which we'd never heard before! Allison also said that photos of Simone from other people would keep coming to us, to remind us of her continued presence in our lives. She mentioned a particular photo Simone loved—it had sunglasses in it and was a 'sisterly' photo—but I couldn't work out which one Allison meant. That night after the reading, I got on Facebook and there was a photo of Simone and Esther that I'd never seen before. It was taken on one of our family holidays, and has the two of them clowning around wearing children's novelty sunglasses and grinning with silly faces at the camera. I have no doubt this is the photo Simone was talking about! It was so like them, and they were very much like sisters.

There were many other parts to the reading that were just as significant and accurate as the ones I've told you about. There is simply not enough paper! One thing I do need to say, though, is that it gave myself and my family insight into how Simone is, where she is and that she is happy. It was validation that I was, indeed, aware of her presence around us, and her small ways of communicating with us and that we are all still strongly connected with her. It doesn't take away the pain of missing her, of feeling she is not here in the way we want her to be, but it helped to know that no matter where we are, no matter what happens, the bond between my sister and I can never be broken. I am forever grateful to have had eighteen precious years with a truly amazing person like Simone as my sister, and to still be blessed with her presence as my guardian angel—and still my sister, just in a different place—for the rest of my life. Allison gave Simone's most significant family and friends the most priceless gift by allowing us to communicate with Simone in a way we never thought possible. We will all be forever thankful to her, for this precious ray of sunshine, in a long difficult journey.

### THE DECEASED'S PERSPECTIVE

Simone, like other young spirits, was on a mission to touch her family in an attempt to lessen their pain. The deceased's ability to be around their loved ones in their homes is absolute but one-sided. Unless the deceased can get the attention of the living, they can only watch the suffering, so it's core that they achieve reconnection. Simone chose to do this through me. Sometimes they use signs that are specific to them, but whether or not the living choose to accept the messages is up to the living. The living have to learn how to see and hear on a spiritual level.

Simone still has work to do, but she's off to a good start. The more people that loved the deceased, the more energy they have to expel to reach them all. The deceased don't mind, though, they see how special they were to so many and it touches their soul.

The love we all have for them fuels them to find a way to show us that they're still a part of our past, present and future.

## Loss of a son

Can you imagine such a horrendous loss? Sadly, parents lose children every day. Michelle shares her experience with you hoping to resonate with other parents who've suffered through losing a child. The only people who truly understands the feelings that pour out of a bereaved parent, are other mourning parents who want to re-connect with their kids.

### My beautiful boy — by Michelle MacMillan

I first saw Allison being interviewed on an Australian breakfast TV show. It had only been about seven weeks since my twelve-year-old son Jack had suddenly and tragically died. I was amazed by her stories and about her father's passing and the visions she had prior to his death. She was doing a show in Sydney that night and I knew I just had to go. I was desperate and excited at the possibility that I might get to connect with my son.

So I went to the Sydney show that night and I was lucky that Allison chose me for a reading. It had only been a short time since Jack had passed, so it was upsetting and emotional, but so very comforting. This began my following of Allison and her incredible gift.

One thing really stood out from her show was Allison's

message that I needed to remember that each day I wake up is another day closer to being with my son again.

On December 7, 2013 I was excited about the opportunity to have a phone reading with Allison. I wanted a longer reading, something just for me and my boy. With the emotion and anxiety in the lead-up to our first Christmas without Jack, it would be the most special Christmas present this grieving mother could ask for.

The first words Allison spoke were that Jack was 'sorry' and 'when he passed he was having difficulty breathing, that he couldn't be saved, there was nothing I could have done and it wasn't my fault.'

He said he could hear people talking around him at the time he was trying to be saved. I remember telling him things like, 'Hold on, Jack, it's okay,' and 'Come on, son, please, breathe'. He could obviously hear me, even though I didn't realize it at the time.

Jack had drowned in our backyard swimming pool. We had only lived in our house for about seven months. When we had been looking at houses, he always asked, 'Does it have a pool?' He was a good swimmer but he knew never to swim without an adult being present. I had been there watching him with his sisters. The girls got out of the pool and Jack stayed in to do a few laps. He was doing some underwater laps, holding his breath to see how far he could go. He'd been doing this with friends and family during the Christmas holidays. Little did any of us know that this common practice which many of us have done over the years would lead to such tragic consequences. We would later learn that something known as shallow water blackout (SWB) had claimed Jack's young life. My precious son had blacked out underwater and it happened so quick it was too late to save him. Jack was a sensitive kid who wasn't a risk-taker, and he'd never have done this if he had an awareness of the dangers. He was a fit, healthy, sporty boy and so his death made no sense, especially as we were unaware something like this could happen, and so quickly and silently. You think when your children are healthy, that you're one of the fortunate ones. I had a false sense of security.

In all three readings I've had with Allison since March 2013, she has always made strong references to how much Jack loved the water, without her having any clue about what happened to him. Allison mentioned how he loved the beach, and photos by the water with the sun in his hair. His grandparents live by the beach and we have many great pictures of him there. We also live not far from the beach and we have friends who also live right by the beach, so Jack has spent a lot of time in the water. Allison told me this is where Jack wants me to picture him, by the water. I wondered if this is why, since his passing, I've had such an incredible sense of comfort when I'm by the ocean and have felt drawn to it like never before.

In the readings Jack kept showing Allison images of him going into the water and swimming, and eventually, in the last reading, she asked if he was particularly attracted to the water. It was at that point that I told Allison what had happened to Jack. She reassured me that he still likes the water and not to see it is a bad place.

Allison spoke of Jack having a strong sister presence and how he spends a lot of time around his sister. I have a daughter

Ella, a stepdaughter Charlotte and my baby girl Liliana with my second husband. Allison was definitely referring to Ella. Jack and Ella were very close, and Ella has told her Dad that she talks to Jack often in her head. Jack wanted Ella to know he is sorry and that he knows it's been hard on her. He wanted her to know that he is her guardian, her caretaker, and that she can have his music! He loved his music and he acknowledged the music we put together for him at his funeral. One of the songs we played was 'Don't You Worry Child' by Swedish House Mafia, a song we used to sing in the weeks just before Jack's death. One of the lines in the song is 'Don't you worry child, heaven has a plan for you'. Sadly this song still brings buckets of tears whenever I hear it playing.

Jack loved his birthday and all of the parties we had. Allison told me that Jack doesn't want his birthday to be a sad day anymore, he wants it to be happy. On the morning before Jack died, he told me that he was going to ask for a Mac and a surfboard for his birthday, which was still another nine months away! He also said he already knew he wanted to have another laser skirmish party for his next birthday when he would turn thirteen.

I was quite overwhelmed when Allison talked about me seeing Jack as my 'beautiful boy'. Since his passing we have often referred to him in this way. His plaque at the cemetery actually has the inscription 'Our beautiful boy' on it. Because of the type of plaque it is, we couldn't have much writing on it, so of all the words we could have chosen, it is quite amazing that Allison mentioned this and it really confirmed for me that she was connecting with my son.

Allison reassured me through Jack's message that I was the best mom and that Jack knows how much I love him, so I don't have to ask him anymore. Since Jack's passing I have had a significant dream where I was sitting next to him with my arm around him, telling him how much I love him and asking him did he realize how much I love him? These dreams are so bittersweet. It's so wonderful at the time, dreaming of my son, until I wake to the shocking reality that he is now gone. Allison acknowledged that this is Jack's way of communicating with me, that he is having a moment with me. Allison spoke of how Jack felt so loved, so happy that I am his mother, but that I was a little 'protective' of my kids! It's true that I have always been overprotective. There was a time I thought I might never have children and then I was blessed with Jack, my first born and only son. I wouldn't even let him cross the road outside our house at twelve years old or walk home from school. He had commented that I was treating him like a baby! Allison said that Jack understands why it bothers me so much that I couldn't save him, and that there was nothing I could have done to change the outcome, it just wasn't meant to be.

Allison made reference to Jack being worried about his grandmother and her health, and how she wishes she could have traded places with Jack. He doesn't want her to think like that anymore, and he loves her, he doesn't want her to say that anymore, that it's not supposed to be that way. My mom had told me her feelings about how she had wished she could have traded places with him, that she wished it could have been her not him. She has had a liver condition for some years now which has affected her health and I guess this had worried Jack. At the reading I had with Allison in Sydney, in February 2014, she mentioned that we should always have a seat for Jack at special celebrations. I told her that my mom had set a place for him at the table at Christmas lunch, our first Christmas without him.

Allison said that Jack had great hair, and he did! Beautiful thick wavy hair that he would spend lots of time trying to get perfect each morning before school. He would get upset if it wouldn't sit properly or wasn't looking quite right. The girls at school had actually nicknamed him Harry, after Harry Styles from the British boy-band One Direction. I'm sure he loved the attention.

Allison mentioned that Jack would be memorialized at his school. I found out a week after the reading that the school had presented the 'Jack MacMillan Sportsmanship Memorial Medal' which would be presented each year to a Year 6 boy in his memory. Jack loved his sports and played competition soccer and cricket. At the Sydney show in 2014, Allison picked up on a boy who was good at everything he tried and in particular sports. I knew it was Jack. In what would be his last cricket season, he was selected for a representative team and he was so chuffed with this achievement.

During the phone reading, Allison and I talked about my sister Sharon, and Jack conveyed that he viewed her as his second mom and how fun she is. He just adored his 'Aunty Shaz'. Allison told me that he was trying to give her a necklace with a heart on it. I explained that I had given my sister a heart pendant with an inscription on it about Jack.

Jack's message to his stepdad was that he was crossing out the 'step' and that he sees Mel as his second father. Jack said that he knows Mel would have saved him if he could, he's sorry they didn't get to spend more time together and he reassured him that everything was going to be all right.

For his father, George, Jack's message was that he loved him very much, and he knows his dad is devastated. He saw his father crying into a pillow, and he's sorry. He said he's never seen his parents in so much pain. He sure is right about that! Jack wanted his dad to know they can still watch TV together and he wants to watch a game with him. I know that this is something that has been very difficult for his dad as they watched a lot of sport on TV together. Jack knows his dad would have made things better if he could have and he wanted him to know 'I'm still here'. Jack also wanted me to make sure his dad knows 'he needs to breathe', that he'll see him again someday and he never failed his son.

It's ironic that Jack expressed how he thinks his death will help save other people and by his dying, other people will live. He knows I wish it didn't happen to him, but he knows if it didn't happen to a great kid like him then people wouldn't care as much. Allison acknowledged that it's sad but true. Yes, it is completely and utterly devastating beyond words and I still do and, always will, question why my beautiful son who still had his whole life ahead of him had to die? Jack expressed that by me having him, he has saved all these other lives. As Allison pointed out, he's now my angel on the other side, helping all the other kids cross over.

Allison said that Jack is going through this journey with me. Every morning he'll be there with me and at night we can still read together. Reading is something that we did every night when he was younger and he continued to do until the day he died. One of the last messages in my reading was that Jack 'pinky swears' he won't leave me and every night when I go to sleep he kisses me on the forehead. He used to 'pinky swear' with his sisters Ella and Charlotte.

It was a truly wonderful Christmas present. Jack brought Allison to me in one of my darkest times of grief and it was the only way he could give himself to me for Christmas. He is my incredible son, who has become an angel way too soon for me to accept, loved by so many and held in our hearts dearly forever. His baby sister Liliana was only six months old when he passed, he just adored her, which I was pleasantly relieved to know, given that I didn't think an eleven-year-old boy would be too fussed about a baby. As Allison said, "He has so much love in his heart, which is rare in a boy his age."

My family has made tireless efforts since understanding how Jack died to educate people about shallow water blackout which tragically claimed Jack's life. If you would like to learn more about Jack's story and SWB, then refer to our Facebook page 'Shallow Water Blackout SWB' or our webpage at www.shallowwaterblackout.org.

Thank you, Allison, for continuing to share your precious gift around the world and for your sincere compassion for grieving parents like me. It's appreciated more than you can ever imagine.

## The deceased's perspective

Bringing kids through for their parents is heart-wrenching but at the same time I'm always amazed at how good their energy feels to me. Their hearts are so pure, and full of love, they make us all better people. Jack had an inspiring energy, he was a pleasure to bring through. Jack's words to his mother came from his heart and his intention to remove his mother's pain was strong. Jack's focus was on his family and the love that they had for him, he was adamant that he was still a part of the family. In Jack's world he has everything he needs because he's with other deceased family members who share their life stories with him, and he's with his living loved ones as well. Jack sees it as his mission to reach each person he loves, so that they don't close the door on communicating with him.

## Across the Pond

I find it interesting that no matter where someone is from in the world, the sentiment in readings is the same. The culture, language and food may differ, but the emotion between the living and the dead is almost identical everywhere I go. It doesn't matter what country I'm touring or calling for a phone reading, the pain from the loss of a child is without measure.

I read a lovely woman from England who had recently lost her son. Her son came through rather easily, and he talked about being around his sister and aunty, and spoke of how he felt at the time that he died. He said his mom had a snapshot of him with all his 'favorite guys', his best friends. I had to laugh when he told me that his friends were all good-looking and that he was a 'beauty snob'; to me, his comment was unique.

The woman's son had reverted to the age of sixteen; he liked that age, he said, as he was able to be close to his family still. He was touched that his mother had kept a lock of his hair. When he told me that he shared his birthday with someone, his mother confirmed, "He shares his birthday with his dad."

The young man said to tell his mom that he loved his 'magic shoes'. I didn't know what this meant, since I'm basically playing charades with the deceased but I passed on the message anyway. Like I always say, 'I'm a glorified secretary to the dead' so when their messages are unclear to me, they're usually personal to the person receiving the reading. His mother explained that these were his favorite shoes, his trainers, that helped him play sports better. He also wanted his mom to know that he was fond of his tree. This was emotional for her, as they had planted one for him after he had died.

But the moment of the reading came when I asked his mother if he had a sports jersey with a number on the back of it, because he indicated loving it. Softly, she shared that she had one made for her son after he died and he was buried in it. This stirred raw emotions in me, I can only imagine how that felt for her to see him wearing his jersey in his casket. Talk about an image that you could never erase from your mind. Although, the pure beauty of a mother caring for her child and being there when he took his first breath as a baby, then tending to him by sewing his favorite jersey for his burial, I was in awe. I felt so honored to even be a part of the moment that they were now sharing. I almost felt like I was intruding on a private meeting, but the 'secretary' needs to be there to pass on the messages to the living.

## The deceased's perspective

As far as I knew that day, I was only supposed to be giving this woman a 'life reading'. But her son had another plan for me, one that involved him. He saw his chance, and he took it. After I introduced myself to her, she started explaining her life questions and they revolved around the loss of her son, almost a year ago. I felt my heart sink, I also heard a voice say, 'You can read her, that's what you do.' Now, normally, I wouldn't conduct a mediumship reading unless the person had attended one of my events. The readings seem stronger for people who understand my process, but all of the sudden my own rules didn't apply. I had the ability to speak for him, and there was no way he was going to let me sidestep doing just that, he wanted me to read his mother, so that she could feel touched by him again, after what must have felt like an eternity. Following that experience, I changed my rule, so that anyone can book a reading. Her son pointed out that it didn't seem fair, since his mother lives in a place that I don't tour. Her son did an impossible thing that day– he changed my mind!

# 7

# Dark endings

*I* know in my other books I've talked about various murders through the minute details of the crime, my predictions and the outcome of the case. Many people are interested in the drama involved with crime but I think it's necessary to think about what happens to the victim, after they die. They don't stay a victim forever.

Here, I want to show you what happens to the victim when they die, how they move on, and find peace. People seem to be under the impression that murder victims become defined by how they died and their killer, but that couldn't be further from the truth. The only ones who freeze-frame the victims in their final moments of life is the living who love them, and that's completely natural because we struggle to understand what actually happened to our loved one, and why. In a sense, we try to walk through every painful moment with the murder victim and somehow share their trauma and fear. By doing this, we become affected by the killer as well, by letting them take us apart emotionally. So although it's natural to try to immerse ourselves in the attack and murder in order to understand what the victim went through, it really serves only to continue the killer's destruction. The murder victims usually prefer to leave the crime in their past, not be forced to relive it.

Murder victims do, however, become very attached to the police officers such as detectives working on their case. This is purely from an emotional standpoint, because they can 'feel' how much the detectives care about them and think about them daily. The relationship that exists between the victim and their law enforcement representatives is very unique; a special one, indeed. The victim can also see how much the detectives care about their family and check up on them, which further endears the detectives to them.

Now, I know this isn't always the case. I've worked with families who have had lackluster relationships with the police, and I've witnessed law enforcement drop the ball, but more often than not, the police give everything they've got to solve a case. Indeed, police officers often take the victims and their family's pain home with them.

When murder victims cross over, they're met by family and friends just like everyone else. Their deceased loved ones usually try to intervene on the victim's behalf and help them to 'leave' their body during the commission of the crime, so that they don't feel all of the trauma.

When I do a reading and I'm asked to bring through a murdered person, it reminds why I do what I do: I'm a trauma specialist, a medium for the murdered, and I wouldn't have it any other way. Some people think that's dark energy to deal with, but in reality, the murdered stand out most often because their light is so bright from within. I get to connect with some of the most beautiful, bright energy, and often it's what attracted the killer to them in the first place. The murderer, on the other hand, has very dark energy. I choose to focus on the bright light, the casualty of bad circumstances.

Murdered people's souls do the same things as all souls do when they pass on: they live their version of heaven. They revert to an age that they were the happiest and the most secure. People who died at the hands of another will never feel fear or pain again, and the killer will never be able to come in contact with them again, not even when the killer dies.

As painful as it is to say, some parents are responsible for murdering their children. However, I've never seen them in a reading with their children. It seems that even if the parent had a chemical imbalance that's now gone, they are somewhere other than with their children. The trauma from the fear involved in the crime seems to act as a barrier, buffering the child from the person who ended their life, even if the killer has regret. My educated guess is that the parent who committed such an unspeakable act reverts to a young age before they were ever a parent, or before their chemical imbalance took a hold of them. So when a chemical imbalance was a contributing factor in the crime, the soul of the now 'well' person will find a sense of calm by living their versions of heaven that occurred in their life before they were unwell.

A victim's soul will find a peaceful place to be; often I'll see them in a pasture stroking a pony or fishing with their grandfather. They show me snapshots of the days when they were happy so that I can relay those positive memories to their living loved ones. They often mention liking all the candles from their memorial, but they don't recognize the heaviness behind the candles; they just see them as a brilliant tribute or, if it's through a child's eyes, they're just pretty candles.

## Only the good die young

Lisa's husband, Barney, was murdered senselessly by a person who didn't consider the consequences of his actions. Imagine being out with your special someone and a reckless soul takes them from you, removes them from your world. When I read Lisa, Barney came through larger than life, happy and full of energy. He stood next to me as I relayed his messages to Lisa and his teenage son. Firstly, Barney thanked everyone for making him music CDs after he died, he indicated that music was a part of who he is. He said that 32 was the age that he reverted to, and Lisa explained that he died at 33. Barney reverted to 32 because that was the last year of his life that everything would be perfect. It was the year that he married his beautiful bride, bought a house, and made a new life. He talked about the two of them at the beach being a version of heaven; Lisa said they went to Jamaica for their honeymoon so I explained that those are the photos he wanted her to display.

Barney mentioned being around his namesake, and Lisa told me that he was named after his father. He also said that he was around the 'crazy dog', which brought a laugh from Lisa. That dog was his 'baby', Lisa said, and indeed crazy.

He showed me things that were very meaningful to him, such as the cross-like religious relic that was for his daughter. Lisa explained, rather sadly but lovingly, that this was a rock with a cross on it, and the only thing that Barney had ever bought for his baby daughter who was unborn when he died. Barney also spoke of 'seeing all the people wear his shirts', which Lisa said referred to a special batch of 'Barney' shirts made for him that were given out to friends and family.

There were many light moments in the reading, too, as Barney's energy was bright. He talked about missing Lisa's cooking. She asked me if the deceased could eat in heaven and I explained that they can, but when the food is made by our hands it carries a more desirable energy. It's more special to them when it's made with love. Barney mentioned his birthday and him wanting a birthday cake—as it turned out, his birthday was the following week and Lisa made sure that he had an amazing cake!

Coincidentally, I wrote Barney's story on his birthday. As I was thinking about him, I remembered that Barney had said at the end of the reading that he'd love Lisa 'always and forever'. It now occurred to me that might be the title of a song that's a sign to her that he's around 'always and forever'. So I sent Lisa a quick message to tell her this. Her reply moved me deeply: Lisa said that, in fact, their wedding song had been 'Forever and For Always' by Shania Twain.

### The deceased's perspective

Throughout the reading, Barney painted us a picture of his version of heaven. He also talked about his kids, how he didn't want his son to close his heart to those he loves out of fear of being hurt again. Barney said that, 'He let everybody in!' This tells us what a big heart Barney has, caring about so many people. He wanted the same for his son, to live a full life. He proudly spoke of his wedding photos being put up, and Lisa said that his son has a very large picture on his bedroom wall of Barney on their wedding day. Barney wanted his son to know that he's always around him, even when he sleeps, and that his father isn't absent but very much *still* his dad.

Barney's motivation to come through in the reading was to help heal his family. In closing, he wanted Lisa to get 'his princess' a necklace from him because, in his opinion, all princesses need bling!

Barney is an example of a man who never should have been taken so young; he was so good, so friendly, and he loved his life. Even after being dealt a bad hand, he remained upbeat and funny, only wanting his family to be happy. From Barney's perspective, he's still with his family and his focus is on letting them know that he's still here. As I write this, the song 'I'm Alive' from the Xanadu movie is blaring from the radio in the background. Message received, Barney!

### Shot in the dark

My younger sister Michelle Dickinson was only 18 when she was murdered from a drive by shooting in South Phoenix on Easter 2009. Michelle was the middle child who had many struggles throughout her life but the last year of her life she completely turned life around when she knew she was going to be an aunt. She crammed two years of school in the day time and evening classes studying cosmetology to live her dream of 'doing the stars hair and makeup in Hollywood'. The night before Easter morning my husband and I took Michelle with several other family members to dinner at the Melting Pot. She was loving all the delicious food. That night we celebrated her belated 18th birthday, a younger sisters 16th birthday, my husband's and mine wedding anniversary along with my in-laws wedding anniversary. It was a fun filled evening with plans for dying Easter Eggs in the morning with my three month old son, Schyler. Michelle couldn't wait to celebrate that holiday with him. My sisters wanted to go out and celebrate their birthdays with some friends. They arrived at the house party but heard gun fire and Michelle attempted to hide behind a pillar when she was struck in the back through her heart and lung. Sadly no killer has been found since the street was littered with gun fire since the people at the party chased the killers with their own guns down the street shooting at the group that started the violence. I miss her laugh, her smile, and her willingness to lend an ear when you need one. She wanted dearly to be a mother and loved being an aunt as she couldn't wait for us sisters to have more babies so that she could love them even more. I miss her goofiness and ironically, her fighting with me over something silly. Now, even more I would let her win if I could get a hug.

When I had a reading at one of Allison's event, I was lucky enough to get picked for a reading. When Allison started talking about how my sister thought of me as her mother, since I raised her and how she was sad for the pain that we all went through with her death being so tragic and unexpected. Allison said that a young woman's spirit was present who was anxious to talk to us. She said that when she passed away, even though it was tragic, she wasn't alone, she said that she had her dad present with her. She said there was nothing that could have been done to save her, that it was just wrong time, wrong place. She said not to beat up our selves for letting her go out.

She talked about how she didn't have any pain and how she was sad for the expense that it caused. Michelle always did worry about others and was always a pleasing soul who wanted to help others. The reading helped me by allowing me to say good-bye in a way that I felt I knew she would get my message, and to hear anything she wanted to say that she wasn't able to since she went so suddenly. I have learned that Michelle would want us to reach our goals, never stop living and keep making memories so that she can be part of it. I constantly talk to her in the car when I have an event coming up, and sometimes it helps me just to know that she is near. If there is a day that I am down and just need to hear from my sister Michelle, her music comes on the radio or my iPod and it just makes me feel her near me with reassurance towards something I am doing. I see some of the same goofiness in my now six year old son. I would tell someone who has lost someone tragically to focus on the person who passed, spend your energy on the person you love. Instead of hating those who caused the pain, it will only make it harder for you to live and make happy memories, we need to embrace those that we lost. They are never really gone, and a way to really keep their memory fresh is for you to celebrate those that are still here and know that by living we take them with us on our journey.

### THE DECEASED'S PERSPECTIVE

Michelle, was very young when she died and being cut down when her life was just beginning is beyond tragic. She loves her family so much that she chose to stay, that is apparent. Michelle must have felt helpless, watching her families' reaction in the first hours after her being shot. There are those of us who will die senselessly and that's frustrating because she didn't need to die, many people don't need to die because of selfish people. Michelle, will spend many moments of her existence living vicariously through friends and family members as they walk down the aisle and, raise their own family. The milestones in life that she missed, she'll sample through others, so that she can experience life's beauty too.

### <u>Murdered children</u>

I can't tell you how devastating it is to see child after child disappear, taken by savages who have no conscience, and to not be able to help them until after they've already been killed. Seventy-five per cent of stranger-abducted kids will be killed within the first five hours. Once someone is stranger-abducted and they're removed from their neighborhood, they have a 95 per cent chance of being murdered. Even though I am a spiritual person, I am also aware that people who rape and murder children cannot be rehabilitated and I believe they should *never* be allowed in society again. I wonder how many victims were a result of an early parole for a violent criminal—scary. Call me old-fashioned but I'd like to see the innocent protected, it's unfair that they have fewer rights than violent offenders.

Children who were murdered show themselves in readings with protective family members on the Otherside who make them feel safe. Usually, they are also with other children who died too soon, who's parents are in the same bereavement group as the murdered child's parents. Children who die really enjoy being around baby animals and family pets, too, Probably because animals are as innocent as children, 'like' energy gravitates to one another.

When I read someone whose child has been murdered, I try and buffer the parents from painful details around the moments of death and instead focus on showing them how effervescent their children are on the Otherside. Instilling joy in the hearts of the injured parties is my focus, and the reason that I can continue to walk this path. Making them feel a sense of peace is not easy to do, but it is possible.

### Suicide

I'd like to dedicate this section to my friend Charlotte Dawson, who took her own life in February 2014. Charlotte was a well-known and colorful media personality in Australia and New Zealand, and was a judge on *Australia's Next Top Model*, among other great accomplishments in her life. A former model herself, Charlotte was very statuesque and glamorous. I met her on the set of Channel 9's *Morning Show* in Sydney, with the energetic hosts Sonia and David. Charlotte was almost intimidating at first because she had such a strong presence, but we soon clicked.

That day I had a hankering for Italian food so one of the show's producers asked Charlotte to make a reservation for Joe and I at Otto's. It was Charlotte's favorite Italian restaurant and she was having lunch there anyway. Otto is a restaurant where people go to be seen, it's right on the water of Sydney Harbour, a breathtaking spot. It was a glorious sunny day and Joe and I lingered there, soaking up a peaceful moment on one of our only days off while on tour. After lunch the restaurant emptied and we were joined by our friend Toby Rand, who's the awesome lead singer for the Australian band Juke Kartel. Then Charlotte sauntered over with a smile on her face and sat with us, too. We all talked for a long time, the sun felt good on my skin, I had a perfect Cosmopolitan cocktail in my hand, and the company couldn't be better.

Charlotte reminded me a little of my close friend Domini, we met in high-school, she was my roommate when I met my husband Joe and she was my maid of honor at my wedding. She sadly passed away, in 2002, from cancer. Domini, was blonde, beautiful and lived in the moment! there was a similar spark there. The connection between us was immediate and strong, and we talked about everything from collaborating on a show together, to the cruelty of people online. Charlotte told me that she was being harassed by strangers online who said callous things and untruths about her (Aussies refer to them as 'trolls'). Being a public figure myself, I totally understood what she was talking about, I've dealt with my share of walking voids. It was nice to have someone to talk to who understands. People wonder why celebrities travel in packs; I think one reason is that we just want to hang out with someone we can relate to, and who isn't going to judge us for standing out.

The restaurant was well past closing, so it was time to say goodbye. I hugged Charlotte and we took a couple of photos together. In one, we made funny faces; I'll never publish that, it's such a special moment that I'm sure Charlotte would want it kept private, just as I do. We made plans to meet in my hometown, Scottsdale, Arizona, the following year on my tour, and as Joe and I left I told him how I felt like I'd known Charlotte my whole life.

A couple of days later I was in Adelaide and I turned on the television and there on the screen was Charlotte, exuding her magnetic energy on *Australia's Next Top Model*. Not long after, Joe's phone rang and it was Charlotte. I thought, *how ironic is that?!*

I was glad to hear her voice again and immediately we started gabbing on right where we'd left off. We talked about show ideas, and projects we'd been working on. At one point she brought up cyberbullying again, and I confessed that I've always pictured the mean-spirited bullies as people who live in their parents' basement, sitting around in their underwear, with no social life. We both had a good laugh at that. But Charlotte seemed like she was pondering something, then mentioned that people online were making fun of her age, which was 47. That got my blood up—anyone who says that's old better remember that one day, if they're lucky to live long enough, they'll be that age, too. As far as I'm concerned, class and beauty have no age. It really angered me that people wanted to bring Charlotte down in that way. I think some of those people might have too much time on their hands.

It was special that Charlotte and I felt that we could confide in each other, the pressures that accompany being a public figure are enormous. There's a lot of perks—don't get me wrong—but you are signing up to be a target for faceless people tapping away on their computers who spread negativity and hate.

But it wasn't all bitching about critics, there was a lot of fun in our conversation as well. We talked about Charlotte coming to visit us, as she had always wanted to go to Scottsdale. She was going to stay with us, and I couldn't wait for my friends to meet her, I knew that they'd love her, too. I was already making plans to take her to El Chorro's in Paradise Valley for sticky buns and mimosas for brunch, and I would be her personal tour guide. It really gave me something to look forward to.

Three weeks later, I came home from a Roberta Flack concert and I was itching to call Charlotte, but the time difference made it too early in the morning. Then the next day our friend Toby Rand contacted us to tell us that Charlotte had taken her own life. I was in shock, and so very sad.

I'm often unable to see suicide, there are too many variables involved, it's not a fated death. A person can decide at the last minute not to suicide, or at the other extreme they can, in a moment, act in haste and decide to end their life; so it's not always clear. I can usually only tell if someone has suicidal tendencies, or if they'll have a short life. Charlotte's energy had 'felt' depressed to me, but I thought she was strong enough to persevere. I was wrong, she was tired of the highs and lows in life, and too wounded.

Everyone's had a moment where they felt like the world was

against them; Joe's always been my rock, he holds me and makes the pain go away. Charlotte didn't have a Joe to save her, but she has a friend named Allison who will not let her be forgotten.

And I'm pleased to say that Charlotte hasn't forgotten me, either! About four months later Joe and I were traveling the east coast of the US for five days. I had an event in Salem, Massachusetts, then we visited friends in New Hampshire. Our friends Jen and Aaron had a work party they wanted us to attend with them, so Joe and I happily tagged along. At one point, Joe and I were sitting on our own on the patio deck at the restaurant; there was a young couple with a baby nearby, but I didn't pay much attention to them. I was gabbing with Joe, my favorite guy, drinking a cocktail, it was a nice moment. Later that night, the baby made its way over to our table, and we met her parents when they came to retrieve her. That's when we learned her name was Charlotte and she was born on my birthday, January 24$^{th}$. Joe gave me that look of understanding—signs are something that we definitely pay attention to in our family!

The next day we were off to Fire Island for a catch-up with a co-writer and his wife, which included another of those relaxing time-outs for Joe and me, drinking Champagne on the patio when we visited their friends. Without warning, their friends' pooch ran out from the house, bounded up and greeted us. "This is Charlotte," the dog's owner said. *Charlotte*? I thought. *No way!*

Celebrities may look strong, but underneath their confidence they're sensitive human beings. They're people who are easily targeted by negative energy, but these days they are also susceptible to cyberbullying. Charlotte became a target for angry people who used technology to hurt her; unfortunately, these unhappy individuals like to share their misery with others. I will remember her as a beautiful, sensitive, energetic force, one that I had hoped to be friends with for a lifetime. 'Til we meet again, Charlotte! No one can hurt you now.'

* * *

If someone you know passed at their own hands, understand that they spend a lot of time observing the rippling effect that their death had on people connected to them, rather than moving on with deceased family members. It is a learning opportunity, because even though people who suicide have a chemical imbalance that lead to their demise, their soul still needs to grasp the aftershock of their actions. The deceased needs to listen to what their loved ones have to say about them, even if it's unpleasant. They have to see that the living blame themselves for the suicide, because they feel they should have seen the warning signs or should have somehow interrupted the deed. Those who commit suicide also need to understand that their loved ones think the deceased didn't love them enough, otherwise they wouldn't have willingly left them. The reason that it's absolutely vital for the deceased to own their actions is because in order for them to become completely whole, they must evolve spiritually, since their chemical imbalance stunted their growth the minute it took a hold of them. This is no fault of the person who committed suicide; when somebody has a chemical imbalance, even with medication and therapy trying to control it, it can still cause a person to do irrational things, which are sometimes fatal.

After a person who commits suicide dies, their chemical

imbalance falls away and they can now see quite clearly. This allows them to fully understand what was going on inside of them, that ultimately led to their demise. Because like energy is attracted to like energy, you will sometimes see one suicide start a domino effect within the deceased's circle of family and friends. Chemical imbalances can be genetic or, alternatively, people are drawn together because of similar energy socially; I have found that this is why it is more prevalent in some families or groups of friends, and not others. It's extremely unfortunate when a suicide sets off a chain reaction, causing a domino effect and devastating families and communities.

When I bring through an individual who passed from suicide, they're initially hesitant with me because they know that I'm going to ask them what happened when they died. So when I feel hesitation from the Otherside, I know there can only be two reasons: either the person died from suicide, or they didn't believe in what I do or their faith looked down on the work of mediums. People who pass from suicide also revert to an age that they felt happy and safe, an age before the chemical imbalance appeared in their energy and took a hold of them. Suicides almost always appear eighteen years old or younger when they come through to me. So when I bring through a man who was in his 50s with grown children but he's appearing around the age of ten, then I know how he passed.

Once they do make their presence known to me, and we've established how they died, they regularly express immediate regret or a feeling of foolishness as soon as they passed. Occasionally, I'll get a soul who never felt like they belonged with the living and they feel relief when they pass, as though they're finally free. The family of souls such as these are often unsurprised to hear of the relief felt by their deceased loved one; they understand and acknowledge that, from the time of birth, their loved one never seemed content or it seemed like there was somewhere else they'd rather be, another time, another place.

### Gone too young

My family lived on 25 acres with my aunt, uncle and cousins in one home and our family in another. We were raised as close to siblings as you could be- without actually being so.

When Allison brought my cousin Joe through, the first thing she said was, "He doesn't want anyone blamed for it. Do you understand!?".

My cousin had been estranged from us for four- years. I put a lot of blame on his parents for not accepting him. I know it wasn't right but it's how I feel. Joe took a bunch of Tylenol and then, attempted to end his life, We found out from a friend of his that he tried to kill himself. Allison told me in the reading that it was because of his head that he died. Well because of the harm he did with the pills he took, he was 'brain dead'. They unplugged the ventilator and his whole family had to watch him expire, at the young age of 26 he took his last breath.

Joe said that what happened to him didn't happen because of a bad upbringing. His parents are to this day some of the most beautiful human beings one could meet. Their life is lived for their children and grandchildren.

Allison said that music was important to Joe and after looking through numerous pictures of us lip-syncing and our family all playing instruments in the band, and,the images of us singing karaoke, this made perfect sense.

Joe was also a disc jockey at numerous weddings, he loved a good party! My mother and Joe would dance all night long at those weddings. I would patiently wait and most nights just before he was done tearing up the dance floor, he would dance with me too. I loved those moments. It's funny, I don't dance much any more. It's as if I am waiting to dance with Joe, one last time.

Allison said that he reverted back to when he was 15 years old. Which I understand as he was very happy at that age. I recently found a picture he had given me (school picture) with a note from him written on the back, he was 15 at the time.

There was a wedding that Allison mentioned and I couldn't remember who's it was, she said we all attended it and Joe was 15 years old. After talking to my sister we figured out it was my uncle's wedding. My cousin Joe was one of the two groomsmen in the wedding party. I have a lot of wonderful memories from that night. It was one of those nights that you'd wish would never end.

Allison said that he loved the tattoos, all of them. At the moment I didn't remember then but after Joe died, my mom got a tattoo for a couple of people who passed away.

Joe was one of them, It read, 'Until we meet again'. There were a few other people who got tattoos for Joe, and I have told them all that he appreciated it.

Allison said, "He loved his family, he doesn't want any doubt about that." That was something I think we all needed to know. I wasn't sure if he meant me, as in, 'he loved his family', even though I am only his cousin. But later in the reading Allison said, "He says he loves you", I felt overwhelmed, it had been a long time since I had heard those words from him.

Allison said, "He did it and when he got to the other side he regretted it instantly."

Allison also said, "Joe says, 'I am ok, I'm fine, stop worrying about me. I'm happy.'"

While watching *What dreams may come* I always worried about where my cousin is at. I would always think of Joe and hope that he was okay. This verified to me where he was and it was a pleasant reassurance.

Allison also asked about the 'beautiful girl' he was referring to, and she asked, "is she yours?" I explained to Allison that I was going to ask about her and I decided to ask about Joe instead. But he said, 'stop worrying about her, I am always with her and I'll keep an eye on her, she will be ok.' We are going in on Wednesday for a diagnosis for my daughter. She is 6 years old and has a delay of about a year (when she was younger it was a delay of roughly 2 years). She was sick one evening (another ear infection) and when heading to her room she started giggling. I know someone was with her, maybe it was him :)

Joe then said, 'thanks for the balloon.' I couldn't for the life of me think of what that meant and then all of a sudden, I remembered my birthday (jan 23) I got a balloon the ones that last a couple of weeks. I looked at my phone and realized at that moment it was 10 years that day that my cousin had passed away. My daughter started crying because the balloon flew away and I said it's ok it is going to the Angels in the sky like Joe and it calmed her down. I said a prayer and in the house we went.

Allison mentioned a beautiful angel with a young or childlike face with big wings, after talking with his mother she said, "that's mine, I have it by my bed and I bought it thinking of him."

Joe has a huge heart, Allison talked about how Joe loved children so much so, now he helps them cross over. There's something quite settling about that, Joe being able to care for children like he cared about me when I was small. I know that Joe's still part of my life, he still guides me and now he watches over my little girl.

## THE DECEASED'S PERSPECTIVE

Joe's intention in the reading was to speak to his cousin and ease her mind. He wanted his cousin Sheila to know that she mattered to him. He needed her to act as his messenger to lighten the hearts of those who missed him. Sheila felt blame for not trying harder to connect with Joe in their adulthood, he was letting her know that there was no need to feel guilty. Sheila's cousin felt responsible for the pain that he brought on through his suicide and he wanted to right his wrongs any way that he could. His intention was to communicate with his loved ones in order to alleviate some of the emotional damage inflicted on his family. Joe's now clear and lucid, so his judgment is much better than when he was alive, since his chemical imbalance is no longer there. He'll find the right time and place to make his presence known to his family, strengthening his relationship with them, until they meet again.

## Forever young

On July 10, 1990 at 5:31pm, a cheeky, mischievous, lovable larrikin and party animal was born ... Joshua Luke Finegan ... and our lives were changed forever. Little did we realize just how dramatically our lives would change, until December 11, 2010, when our darling, cheeky, mischievous and lovable Josh took his own life.

Josh was our darling son, our special and beautiful boy. He was an adored brother and best friend to Amy and was a much loved and cherished nephew, cousin, great mate, friend, bro and buddy, and he had the ability to touch people's lives in so many special ways. He was intelligent, outgoing, spontaneous, cheeky, mischievous, impulsive, confident, frustrating, talented, passionate and fearless and always managed to bend the rules to suit himself. He was always up for a challenge and willing to try new things and he had a unique zest for life. His vibrant and spirited personality always managed to put a smile on everyone's face no matter what. He was extremely witty and funny and he could think very quickly on his feet. He was a scallywag and a lovable larrikin. He lit up a room when he walked in. He made our world a more beautiful place to be.

Josh loved life! He was the life of the party and would seize every day, but he was also a risk taker, impulsive at times, loved a drink with his mates and was in a tumultuous relationship. And when we looked closely at the risk factors involved in suicide we discovered that Josh did in fact fall into that high risk category. Impulsivity mixed with alcohol and a relationship fraught with dramas appears to be a common causal factor with our young.

Our lives completely fell apart when Josh died and we

constantly questioned and tortured ourselves as to how something so devastatingly tragic and sad could be happening to us. Josh had no history of depression or mental illness. He had the job of his dreams working as a flight attendant; he had just bought his first car, he was appointed captain of his AFL footy team and he was in a live-in relationship with his girlfriend. But how and why does suicide become an option? How does it enter ones realm of thinking? We just don't understand that at all.

The thing that deeply saddens us now is the absolute waste. We knew that Josh would have grown into a fine and successful young man. He would have realized that there is life after a broken relationship and I have no doubt he would have found his soul mate. A lot of his friends are now at the age where they are getting married. He will never get to experience that. We will never get to be grandparents to his children. We will never get to see where his journey would have taken him. We feel so very sad for Amy as well because she now has to live her life without having her brother to grow old with and to share things with. She and Josh were extremely close and like us, she misses him terribly. She will never get to be an aunty to Josh's children and share family gatherings where their kids would have played together. All of the things that you take for granted and assume will happen in the normal scheme of things are what we now miss the most. We would do anything to have the old days back.

After Josh died, it was very important for us as a family to be able to talk openly about our very special boy, because he did live, and he was an extremely happy, positive, cheeky, charismatic and fun loving person. Little did we know that his death was to have such an incredible and indelible effect on so many people and his life has left imprints in so many hearts, most of all mine.

However, talking openly about suicide is incredibly private and difficult, and so stigmatized, that as a society we desperately avoid doing so, thus continuing the secrecy and shame. Until one has a direct experience of the loss of a loved one or friend by suicide, it is possible to go through life unaware that more people die this way than through car accidents.

Josh, will always be our beautiful boy who will forever live on in our hearts, our minds, our memories, our thoughts, our words and our actions. He brought so much love, laughter, happiness and joy to all our lives and we miss him every minute of every hour of every day. Our pain is constant, relentless and always there, and no words can convey the emptiness and sadness in all our hearts. But our lives have gone on. We are surviving and functioning, some days I don't really know how, but we do.

Approximately six-months after Josh died I heard that Allison were coming back to Australia at the end of 2011. I desperately wanted to ensure that we bought tickets to your show as I had read all your books previously. I managed to buy VIP tickets for Amy and I as well as my sisters and nieces living in Brisbane. Not sure what to expect when we attended I just knew that if Josh wanted to connect with us he would do so at your show. So it was a relief when Joe picked Amy out of the audience. You were able to tell us that Josh was the comic of the family and could think very quickly on his feet and reply with great humor. You said, that the number 16 was featured prominently and that was his football jersey number, so that was very significant. You stated that Josh was a ladies man and he broke a lot of hearts when he died. You told me that as a mom I used to lie beside Josh when he was younger and now he lies beside me at night and tucks me in. He wanted us to know that he is happy and at peace and by the beach and he did not want us to be sad. He hated seeing us cry. You said that his suicide was more of an accident rather than carefully planned and that you did not think Josh actually intended to die, but being so drunk and angry he would not have thought his actions would be final. You quoted that the events that led up his death resembled 'the perfect storm'. He did not consciously think that he would not wake up again the next day. You also mentioned a special necklace that I wear. (I had a crystal heart pendant with a lasered photo of Josh made for Amy and I). You also mentioned tattoos. Josh had 1 small tattoo on the outside of his right foot which said *'Seize the Day'*. My husband, Amy and I all had matching tattoos done the week prior to your show. You told us that Josh wanted us to go on living. He said that Amy now has to be the anchor of the family and that he liked it when she wore pink. He also said that he had met Amy's son, his nephew, and he would be named after Josh and he would send him to Amy when she was ready.

What you told us that night was very powerful and thought provoking but most importantly it greatly assisted Amy with her grieving. It provided us with some comfort and reassurance, the reading reinforced in us the importance of believing and having hope. It validated things that had been churning through our minds.

It is now just over four years since Josh died and we continue to miss him every minute of every hour of every day. I miss everything about him. I miss not seeing him, not talking to him, laughing with him, yelling at him, listening to him, sharing thoughts, experiences and dreams. A huge part of me died with Josh.

I hope that by sharing our story that maybe someone reading this will think twice about taking their own life then something positive will have come out of our tragedy. Only today in our State newspaper there was a story about 2 prominent and up and coming football players who died by suicide over the last weekend; One being 18 years of age and the other 20. Just so incredibly and terribly sad. I would not wish this journey on anyone.

### THE DECEASED'S PERSPECTIVE

Josh didn't mean to end his life, his judgment was clouded by alcohol. When people die in this kind of situation, they're often mad at themselves because they had more life to live. They want a way back to their life but realize it's not possible. The details of their death is hard for them to see and hear, because they weren't really ready to go. Josh being a young man has a lot of energy on coming through, young people are more fueled to connect with the living because the emotional wounds run deeper than when say, the elderly die. The elderly are somewhat prepared to die, they lived a full life and enjoyed all the stages of life. Young people had a limited experience, so the grieving have a hard time letting go of the dreams they had for their children, grandchildren, or any young family member. Josh wants to remain a part of his family, he will attend weddings, holidays, births, and play with the babies in the family. He'll stay in the house with his parents and be there when they die, so that he can wrap his arms around them and take them home.

## An exceptional event in San Jose, California

At one of my ballroom events, in San Jose, California, I brought through a man who had committed suicide. We'll call him 'Kent' and he started out solemn and apprehensive. After a few minutes he lightened his energy and was even trying to be 'playful' with his fiancee, her sisters and friends, who had all come together for the event. I usually advise people to wait at least three months after the death of a loved one before they get a reading; this is not because of the deceased, they come through just fine, it's because of the living who are still so raw from the loss. Kent had only died six weeks prior to coming through, so a part of him was in denial and still acting as though he was alive. He even compared himself to Bruce Willis' character from *The Sixth Sense*, and he was aware that he hadn't yet fully accepted his death by suicide. Kent felt bipolar to me, so I understood what led to his suicide, and his fiancee confirmed that he suffered this condition.

Despite the short timeframe, Kent came through because he wanted his fiancee to know that he was okay and that her life had a lot of meaning, so she should go out there and live it. He also wanted her to know that his passing had nothing to do with how much he loves her, that she couldn't have prevented it. It was his cross to bear, not hers. At least, that's how he saw it.

Kent's apprehension to come through is common, so is his

relief once he's reconnected with the living. Suicide isn't like other types of passings because the deceased 'chose' to die, so this creates tension between the living and the deceased. Once messages have been exchanged, it 'clears the air' between the two parties, and the deceased's energy lightens, finally feeling free from the guilt they had carried from the manner that they passed.

No matter how we die, as long as you have a soul and empathy for people around you, we end up in the same place. Which is, wherever you want to be. Like energy gravitates to like energy on the Otherside. Good people will interact with those who touched their lives even in the smallest measure. People who pass from suicide will be reunited with family and friends just like everyone else.

I have come across deceased people who had no conscience, no empathy in their soul; murderers, molesters, nefarious souls. They end up separated from those they hurt. Since vacant souls always put their own needs first, they end up on a different energy plane than everyone else. The energy of the Otherside seems to act as some sort of protection for people who were violated in their life. I've never seen a victim and their killer around each other, even if they were related. I've brought through several vacant souls and they acknowledge their actions, but they seem to lack the ability to care. They don't show themselves being around family and friends because they're not in the same place. They always show themselves alone, so either they prefer to be alone or their isolation is all that they deserve.

As for the rest of us, we all get to pop in and visit our living loved ones, we can relive our happiest days as if they are happening for the first time. And we get to spend time around family and friends who died, catching up and reflecting on our lives. On the Otherside, color is more vibrant, music is sweeter, laughter carries for all to hear, and we experience a sense of contentment that we never felt in life. If you had loved ones who weren't so happy in life, they are now filled with the happiness that they craved, in the afterlife. This is most likely because, negative energy, or the baggage that we collect in life, doesn't seem to transfer to the afterlife.

## But ... I'm religious

A number of people with strong religious convictions contact me, and they feel torn between what they *feel* is true and what they're taught. That's got to be very confusing when you want to connect with the Otherside. It's my belief that you don't have to choose between believing in the afterlife *or* your religion; they can co-exist. Spiritual people are actually extremely easy to bring through in a reading because their energy knows how to function spiritually. Some religions, however, translate in the afterlife better than others. It could be because the devout believers choose to go through a medium from their own religion or they may just not have anything to say. For the record, Jewish moms are fun to bring through, but people of various faiths come through all the time with amusing stories and jokes. It all depends on how they lived and loved, that's what determines how much force is driving their ability to communicate with the living. Those who embraced the people in their life and helped their fellow man, they come through with no problem!

I experienced a moment of enlightenment that I want to share because it might help people of religion to understand that people with abilities are often religious themselves. Religions includes spirituality much more often than religions excludes it. I think people often get confused and think that connecting with the souls of our loved ones isn't okay or it's not possible, when nothing could be further from the truth..

I like to reflect on a dinner that I had years ago as a teaching experience, since I'm often asked about religion and spirits. I once had dinner with a Catholic priest—who's a medium. I saw it as a chance to ask all the questions I've ever had about being a medium who also believes in God. It was an incredible opportunity brought about by a mutual friend who organized for us all to meet.

At first, though, I admit I was a little defensive. As I sat down next to him, I thought about how the idea that a priest could also be a medium could create such a conflict of beliefs, I believed it was possible for a medium to be a priest, you just don't hear it very often.

The Catholic church hasn't always seemed like the biggest fan of mediums, at least that's what I have heard from clients over the years. Although, I have to say they seem more open minded than some of the other faiths. Some faiths come right out and call us messengers of the devil himself! On the flip side, Buddhism, Hinduism, Shinto are very spiritual religions, many religions are spiritual and encourage staying connected to our ancestors. I believe that people of any religion can be spiritual if they choose to stay connected to their deceased loved ones. I toured Japan once, I enjoyed Japan quite a bit, they have shrines to their ancestors and they honor them daily. I was on a press tour there for my television show *Medium* and they totally understood and respected my ability to communicate with spirits.

Anyways, I asked the priest, "How do you balance your religion with being a medium? How do you reconcile what you teach with what you know inside to be true?"

The priest explained to me that there is interpretation in reading the Bible and he finds that his beliefs line up most of the time with what is written there.

Then before I could stop myself I blurted out, "People who commit suicide don't go to hell." (I couldn't believe I'd said that out loud. Me and my big mouth.)

I expected him to refute me but instead he leaned closer and said, "I know, I see them, too. I counsel both the living and the dead."

Now my head was really spinning as I tried to make sense of this one. "So does that mean you're not going to call me the Antichrist?" I asked and laughed.

"Not unless I'd apply that same term to myself," he said.

The priest and I spent a few moments studying each other, and both of us had a bit of a smirk. His eyes were cool and contemplative. He almost seemed relieved to have another person like him to talk to. I had so many questions to ask him. This was an opportunity that most mediums never have, to speak to a priest who understands what it is to be a medium.

He shared a story from his childhood that included him attending parochial school and a nun who worked there who seemed to understand his path. He had questioned her about animals that die and his belief that they were in heaven.

She responded, and I paraphrase, 'If we love animals, then God loves them, too, so why wouldn't they go to heaven?' The father explained to me that this form of belief is called 'theology from below', meaning common sense of the faithful people. I found this all extremely interesting and enlightening. I think that was a good answer from the nun, an honest, gentle response for a child.

We talked about many things that night, and he had questions for me, as I did for him. He wanted to know why sometimes the deceased appear in our heads and sometimes they appear in front of us. A spirits ability to communicate depends on how much energy the spirit has to come through clearly. This is usually determined by the life the person lived. If people knew how to connect to others emotionally in life, that carries over in their spirit and allows them to still reach the living easily as they did when alive. If people were isolated or didn't care for others in life, then that also carries over, and they will still have a difficult time communicating. It takes spirits far less energy to appear in our head than before our eyes. People who had really fun, dramatic, loving energy come through with more ease than someone who was confused, had trouble connecting with others emotionally, and didn't communicate well. It doesn't mean that one was bad, it's just an energy issue, and a question of whether the deceased have the ability to express their energy well enough to reach the living. The father said that he found my explanation reflected his own experiences.

I wanted to go back to the topic of suicides and the Catholic faith, so I asked: "Father, you say that you know suicides cross over, too. Do you believe that God would punish people with chemical imbalances as though they were in control of their actions?"

"No," he said. "I know people who commit suicide go to a good place to be with their family and friends. I see them. Sometimes they seek me out. God knows chemically imbalanced people are trying to deal with their own pain and they sometimes act in haste."

He went on to tell me that the church no longer takes the stance that those who commit suicide go to hell, and it hasn't for more than 30 years. The church allows that people who commit suicide are not in control of themselves, that they are ill, and as such God doesn't punish them for it. I don't know if this information is widely known. People still seem to think that those who commit suicide aren't 'heaven-bound'. It's good to know that they are looked at by the Catholic church with understanding and compassion.

As we were talking about his religion's view of mediums, I asked him, "Weren't we created in God's image?"

"Yes, Allison," he replied, "we all were."

"And didn't Jesus himself appear to people after his death?"

"Yes, he did, and King David, too. David appeared to a woman who summoned him after his death. It's in the Bible. This also testifies to the notion that life after death is possible. Not only to exist after your body dies, but for the living to communicate with those who've passed away." He added with a smile, "Allison, I'm already sold on the fact that we're eternal."

Then he continued, more somberly: "The church acknowledges that mystics truly exist, but the church worries about evil spirits being able to be brought through by mediums. That's a concern."

I had to agree with him there; unethical mediums are a concern. Still, I countered, "Father, I've never brought through anyone who's hurt anyone after death, have you?"

He said he hadn't.

I told him, "I witness evil more in the living than in those who are on the Otherside." I used the example of being at a murder trial, when I'm sitting within arm's length of evil, I often see the defendant sit there with a smile on his or her face while witnesses testify how they saw the defendant carry out a cold-blooded killing. "I'm more worried and shaken by them than I am by any spirit," I said.

As our conversation continued, the father and I agreed that all babies are born in the image of God, but as we get older, we can find darkness within ourselves that we either embrace or try to change for the better.

I also wanted to ask him about the term 'false prophets', it's something I'd been wondering about, whether the church meant people who *pretended* to predict or commune with the dead, or *all* mediums. The priest explained that false prophets were "people who don't actually have these abilities and are pretending to be a mystic not to help others but to harm them."

I'm glad I cleared that up, because it tells us that the church doesn't view mediums as bad. It believes that people who aren't what they claim to be are 'false', and the church has a dim view of those people.

I can't begin to tell you how much I enjoyed meeting and 'breaking bread' with such a rare man of the cloth. But I wondered, is he really so rare? I bet there are many people of God who can communicate with those who've passed on. However, I ultimately decided that, yes, this priest is rare, because he's willing to understand and own both his priesthood and his mediumship abilities.

As I took in the significance of this validation, I realized that it's the true that anybody can be cut from the medium cloth, anybody at all—a mother, a child, a priest, anyone.

Because it's human and natural to connect with people we love, even after someone's physical body dies their spirit remains and is stronger and clearer than ever. I am a student of life just like everyone else, I took a lot away from that day, a conversation that will help shape who I become. It is comforting to me to know that throughout the Bible there are mentions of spirits appearing before the living and communicating with them. It's also reassuring to know that there were many mediums who came before me, and there will definitely be many who come after me.

After I said goodbye to the priest and left the restaurant, I turned to my friend and told her how taken aback I was. I still continue to learn from that unique experience.

\* \* \*

As far as religion goes, how is it so different when a medium asks to be believed, in that we can see something that may not be visible to others? When you hold the reality of being a medium next to that of a man of religion who's asking people to believe in a God that can't be seen, it's not so different. Both claims center around one's belief and personal spiritual experiences. Both are leaps of faith.

I believe in a higher power, I believe I'm being taught many lessons in my life, and I'm paying attention to absorb all that I can while I'm here. I'm not minimizing anyone's religion. I'm just drawing a comparison of the two faiths. Often the faiths overlap, as they should, because both focus on something that gives us hope and healing.

Being a compassionate person and embracing people when it's not the easiest thing to do or the most convenient time to do it are tests of character both, spirituality and the basis of religion promote good character. We should all strive to help others, to love those around us and pray for those who need it. If this chapter allows a grieving person to embrace the afterlife by alleviating their religious guilt around spirituality, and ultimately provides them with peace then spirituality and religion have worked together for the same goal. .

# Bereavement

> The only walls that are built between us and the Otherside are constructed by the living.
> — Allison DuBois

## THE SIX STAGES OF GRIEF

*I* know that many bereavement counsellors believe there are five stages of bereavement, but I believe in six. These six stages of grief are—denial, anger, bargaining, depression, acceptance and reconnection. Reconnection is the stage that most counsellors don't include, but for me, and for those I bring through, it's the most important step to overcoming the grief of losing a loved one.

## Denial

I experienced this myself when my dad, Mike, passed away. He died suddenly, so there was no preparing to lose him but rather I was slapped in the face by the phone call telling me that my dad had died. My response was, "You mean my grandma died."

As I sat on the plane to go to Phoenix to make Dad's funeral arrangements, I still thought, 'This has got to be a mistake, he's healthy, he's been a ballroom dancer for 50 years.'

And even as I looked at my dad in the casket, I couldn't grasp that the person I was looking at was really him. My dad was so full of life, and the man that I saw wasn't laughing, or able to cha-cha as he walked.

My denial started to fade, but there were still mornings when I would wake up and think that it was all a bad dream. I would pick up the phone and dial his number, hoping that he would answer; he didn't. Some people who are in denial will continue to live their life, but make it all about the deceased and ignore other family members; that can be very hurtful to the living family members, who feel invisible.

You know in your mind that your loved one is deceased, but your heart won't accept not seeing them again. So a struggle between reality and wishful thinking ensues, until you no longer have the energy to fuel your inner conflict. Once you're exhausted, reality sets in, and stays like an unwelcome house guest. You place their things in front of you and hold their house keys, their comb, the last note in their wallet that they took out of the bank right before they died. You pour over their daily items, as you probe them with your fingertips, trying to feel your loved one's energy.

## The deceased's perspective

Think of the deceased as they helplessly watch us struggle with their loss. They walk with us through our stages of grieving, knowing that we need them for strength. So not only did their physical life end, but now they feel responsible for our dying inside because of them. They see our denial, they see us reach for them, they see us pick up the phone to call them. But the deceased aren't provided the luxury of denial, they're very aware of who's among the living and who exists in spirit. My father had to see me fall a part as I tried to convince myself that he wasn't really gone. He probably wanted to be on the other end of my phone call to a ghost, so that he could answer me and make my anguish disappear. 'Denial' is a stage that fights to give us moments of peace as we begin a very long journey back to our deceased loved one.

## Anger

I was angry with God, in church I told God that I wasn't going to talk to the dead anymore, I wasn't going to do the work that he wanted me to do, because he took my dad. Why not take a pedophile? A murderer? Why did it always seem to be the good ones who paid the price? I was also angry with family members who had previously stressed out my dad; maybe all of the years of stress caused his heart attack? I was mad at Joe for loving me, I didn't want to care about anyone who could leave me so completely destroyed if I lost them. When you hit your anger phase, nobody can reason with you, because your emotions are too raw. I used to scream, 'I want to rip the roof off heaven and bring him back!'

For me, denial and anger were acting in concert. The effects were already obvious on the plane ride home, when my dad had been dead for less than 24 hours. A woman wanted the window seat next to me, and though I was barely functioning, I bent my knees and pulled my legs up on my seat so she could get pass. She said, "I'd prefer that you stood up!"

I told her, "I'd prefer that my dad wasn't dead!" She sat somewhere else.

When a person is going through the anger phase, they often lack an edit button, they misplace their tact, and this is very normal. So if it happens to you, don't beat yourself up, it's a part of processing grief. Just try not to break any laws while processing. I found that anger was more than a phase, it was a re-occurring emotion that was peppered throughout the grieving process— until you're ready for stage six, reconnection.

## The deceased's perspective

The anger phase is hard for them to watch. They knew you as the happy, loving person in their life, and now you're difficult to recognize. They want you back the way you were before; before they died, before all of the pain. The deceased move through the stages of grief with you, it helps them to process their physical death as well. So, in essence, you're going through it together, side by side. My father knows that I can be a willful person, so the 'Anger' phase must have made him cringe. I'm not very good at keeping my feelings bottled up inside of me. When you're going through the anger, you become a live wire and you affect everyone around you. I know that my dad understood my pain, but imagine having to watch your child be torn a part by your loss. The grieving can't be reached by the Otherside when we go through the anger phase, so they kick it in to high gear to get messages to you any way they can. My dad stood beside me as I watched women twice my age laugh with their dad over lunch. You're not angry at others for having what you no longer do, you just don't understand why you had to be one of the living who feels robbed by death. Everyone takes a turn losing someone they love, it just happened to be my turn.

## BARGAINING

I think most people try to bargain with God. I swore that if God brought my dad back, I would only do good, I would keep doing the work and we could forget about all the pain in my heart, the lump in my throat and the knot in my stomach. Bargaining doesn't work, but you have to try because you love the deceased person so much. Bargaining is a strange place to find yourself, your desperation to hold on to your loved one overrules your mind that tells you that bargaining won't work.

### The deceased's perspective

The bargaining phase makes the deceased shake their head, they know it doesn't work, and they know this is the one time that most people talk to God, to try to strike this unnatural bargain. For me, bargaining was my shortest phase; I knew once I made my demands clear to God that I was on my own on this one, and I quickly moved on to depression. Bargaining usually takes place right after our loved one dies. The grieving will try anything to bring their loved one back. Bargaining is born out of desperation and love. My dad had to witness my painful plea to a higher power as I tried to will him to stay. He would have felt helpless and sad watching me struggle, knowing that there was no other way for me to heal. Grieving is natural and necessary but, it's a long process that is emotionally taxing. Our deceased loved ones lend us their energy to give us a push forward and even then you're not sure if you'll have enough strength to move on with the living.

## Depression

Oh, the deep level of sadness that you feel! You feel dead inside, you walk around in a heart-wrenching fog, waiting for something to change inside of you. You take inventory of your memories, making sure that you remember every single thing about the person you've lost. Your depression makes you push away everybody who cares about you, you don't want to be loved anymore. The dark depth of depression can consume you, you'll cry at the drop of a hat, or the mention of their name. You wonder why you're here at all. You feel guilty if you laugh, and you put yourself in a depressing corner for even thinking of feeling good.

Depression is a very hard phase to move through, it's like walking on broken glass, and you'll have the scars to prove that you didn't walk out of the loss unscathed.

I've noticed that a lot of grieving people in this phase go to Disneyland, and so I did the same thing with my family after my dad died. I know that might sound strange, but when all you feel is sorrow, you think that maybe 'The Happiest Place on Earth' can remind you of what life is about. Instead of sitting in your house and staring at the wall, you sit on a park bench and watch children play. You see the pride on the parents' faces as they take snapshots of their family, the little beings that they love the most in this world. Taking my family to Disneyland helped to pull me out of my paralyzing haze of sadness. As I sat watching our three girls laughing, beaming, living, it reminded me that's what I was to my dad. I was that when he was alive, and I am still that to him now. The warmth that fills a parent's heart, that's us, let's give them something to smile about.

## The deceased's perspective

It's tough for our deceased loved ones to witness our depression. They feel for us, yearn to take our pain away. They hear our thoughts and they see us stumble as we grapple with their loss. I use to sit in my car and listen to Karen Carpenter sing Solitaire, I'd play it on repeat and cry missing my dad. He saw me. Throughout my depression my dad was there, he saw me mentally check-out, he saw me push Joe away. He watched me smile trying to enjoy Christmas three months after he died, even though I was crying on the inside. His birthday was Christmas Eve, I had a party at an old haunt of his. Sometimes alcohol helped to not feel, so I got through his birthday alright. He saw how much he was loved, he realized what a big part of our lives he was. All he could do, is watch and try to talk to a daughter who wouldn't be able to hear him for another few years, because her wall of pain was impenetrable.

## Acceptance

Acceptance is a double-edged sword—you're able to move forward, but you feel like you're moving away from them. Acceptance can feel quite empty, because you feel as though you've given up the battle to hold on to pieces of their soul. In reality, though, you're moving towards them.

When you get to the part where you can accept your loved one's passing, I recommend that you immediately begin the process of reconnection. Once you've accepted their physical death, you can start to really interact with their spirit. Acceptance is key when it comes to communicating with them in a whole new way. Now it's time to memorialize them with joy, and you slowly start to hear and feel a soft voice speaking to you within your heart. The more you talk to them about your day, the louder the voice becomes, and as it gets louder, you'll find that your heart begins to heal.

When you do things that they loved in life, like listen to their favorite music, make their favorite dinner or any activity they loved, you intensely feel their energy around you. Acceptance allows you to rebuild your life, with them spiritually being a big part of your everyday experiences. We get to bring them with us through life, they can share in your laughter, your victories and, yes, your defeats as well. They can be there for you, and buffer your setbacks, they have the power to lend us their energy when we need it, when we think we can't get through a hard time, they give us that extra little push!

## THE DECEASED'S PERSPECTIVE

After the first year, acceptance is forced on you, you can no longer pretend that they're on a cruise or away on business. The second year hits you hard, acceptance knocks the air out of you, literally. The deceased know that acceptance is painful for us but they know that it's necessary. Without acceptance, they can't access us to communicate. They hold our hand through this phase. For me it became easier to feel my dad around me once I was thrust in to acceptance. Even after 'acceptance' you have your good and bad days. Some days I was able to see the beauty around me, other days, everything was grey and felt without meaning. My dad watched me miss out on a number of days with my babies because I couldn't quite function. At about that time, *Medium* came out, It had been two years and three months since my dad died.

## **Reconnection**

After acceptance, comes reconnection—when you begin to reach for the spirit of the deceased from within. Every fibre of your being is prepared to receive a 'visit', and you're open to signs from your loved ones, and you begin to acknowledge both the spirits and their signs.

Once you have arrived at this phase, your healing truly begins, and you feel it so strongly. Your pain starts to morph into a peaceful knowing—knowing that they're still a part of you, and your life. You will now look forward to the signs, and smile when you get them, as you whisper a 'thank you' to your loved one for coming through for you. Their birthday is no longer such a sad day, but a day to celebrate their life and the happy times you shared. There will be an understanding that they're not in some ethereal place, but beside you, talking to you, touching your hand and loving you. Reconnection puts you on the same page energetically, and accelerates the healing. The deceased don't want you to miss out on life, feeling like you died inside, too; it's not what they want at all. They want you to thrive and show them the world through your eyes. You now give them bragging rights on the Otherside, as they point out to others that your connection is so cohesive and solid, that your bond is unbreakable. This also has a positive effect on other deceased people, sending a ripple of energy through the spirits around them and encouraging them to try harder for their own reconnections.

## THE DECEASED'S PERSPECTIVE

Our deceased loved ones welcome reconnection. Having followed us through the previous stages of grief, they are relieved when we are ready to talk to them again. Imagine the joy that both the grieving and the deceased feel when the lines of communication are re-established. Finally, they can show themselves to us, talk to us, and we are capable now of recognizing the signs that they work so hard to send us. It's not that they hadn't sent signs before, the grieving are often blocked by pain and unable to recognize the signs. Reconnection heals and soothes us, eases us back into a comfortable place—a place that feels like home, one with them still in it.

My re-connection came about four years after my dad died. I had already received obvious signs and many messages through other people, including my three year old. My day came when I was at the mall, I stopped to look in the store window, my dad's reflection was looking back at me. Re-connection, he knew he'd made contact with me then. He looked so relaxed, so content, all I could do was stand there staring at him. Even though he was there and I was looking right at him, I wanted so badly to touch him, but being a medium I knew this could only be accomplished from within now. I've since found peace as I move towards seeing my dad again. I can hear him talking to me, calling me 'Jellybean' like when I was small. I hear him more than I see him, probably because instinctually children get upset when they see their parent and, we want to run to them, like when we were toddlers. So my dad talks to me more often than appearing to me, as to not cause me any more pain. My dad is still in my life, it takes more than death to sever our ties to those that we love.

# 9

# Relationships

### WHAT IS LOVE?

*I* write a weekly advice column for *New Idea*, a national women's magazine in Australia; I also answer a lot of relationship questions at my events and in readings—after all, our lives revolve around those we love. You'd be amazed at what people will ask me when they're not thinking clearly. At my events, I tell people to not ask me if they should get a divorce if their spouse is sitting next to them! I also ask that they not question me about their relationship if there's a mother-in-law sitting with them, because she might throw them under the bus! I joke with my audiences but there's also truth to these statements.

There are a lot of broken hearts out there, and I act as the wise big sister who will tell you exactly what my take is, if it will help to guide you out of the fog that your relationship has left you in.

I believe that there is someone out there for just about everybody, with the exception of serial killers and sociopaths, of course!

## THE ONE WHO GOT AWAY

When we're young and fall in love, we always assume that our life will send us another mate, should the relationship we're in not work out, but that's not always the case. A lot of the letters that I get are from people who, twenty or more years later, never got over their first love. They want to know if they should reach out to the one that got away. My advice is, if you're not married, then of course you should reach out! Keep in mind that it might not be like it was when you were eighteen, and they may look a little different, but you share memories and a past, that is unique so take a chance on love. Life is too short to wonder 'what if'. If you sit on the sidelines too long, hesitating, you might find out that somebody else is now living the life that you could have had. I always admire people who keep searching for love, they're more likely to find it than those who assume that it's not out there for them. People shouldn't measure themselves by the relationships in their lives that didn't work, failed relationships just make you appreciate your love story when it comes along, so much more.

## INFIDELITY

I'm always amazed at how many people deal with a cheating spouse—those scoundrels! I'm of the opinion that it's better to get a divorce than a venereal disease from your husband's mistress! There are a lot of variables in a relationship—children, money, your heart, too many to count—but I know that there are countless loving, good people out there waiting for their turn at happiness. From what I've seen, most people who are serial cheaters keep doing it until they get too old to expel the energy.

I've gotten letters from women and men who've spent 40 years being cheated on, and that makes me sad to think that the book of their life will have a running, rocky storyline. So when I get a letter from a young person in the same situation, I tell them to throw that fish back in the sea!

I also get letters from those who are in cheating relationships asking me if they should have a baby. Really?! I think that bringing a child into a broken relationship is a selfish thing to do. That's just my little ole opinion. If your biological clock is ticking, you have some options these days!

Having a baby will never save a relationship, it will only complicate it. Kids also emulate what they see growing up, so there's a good chance that they will cheat themselves or have low self-worth and date someone who reminds them of the cheating parent. That's a lot of baggage to be born with, don't you think?

## LOVE LETTERS

In this chapter I wanted to include examples of some of the common relationship problems that people ask me about—maybe some of you have similar questions. I'm hoping to save those in complicated relationships from wasting their days on people who are most likely a lost cause. Some of you will roll your eyes at these dilemmas, and others will find themselves in a similar situation.

\* \* \*

I have been with my boyfriend for about three and a half years. I am 51 years old, he is 61 years old. He is very mixed up. He has work problems, he is president of local club, he is trying to sell his house and then divorce his wife. He says he loves me, but he can't resist his mates for drinks. He lives with his elderly aunty and I hardly see him. I love this guy, when we're together we're so happy, but its feels like he is being tugged from all angles. He says that once he sells his house and divorces his wife, all of this will change. Am I being selfish or should I just sit back and wait? Can you please help?
Regards, 'hopelessly in love with a mixed-up person'.

*In my experience, I've noticed that when a person wants to be divorced, they get divorced. It seems to me that your boyfriend surrounds himself with women who fulfill different needs in his life. His aunt is his stability, and she provides him with the freedom to blame 'having no time' on taking care of her. Your boyfriend wants to do what he wants, when he wants, and he answers to nobody.*

*He has a wife, plain and simple. If I were you, I'd tell him to give me a call when he's divorced! Otherwise, he's going to string you along forever. Remember that he's the one causing the friction and blaming it on others, he's calling all the shots, don't let his passive aggressive behavior get the best of you.*

*It might be time to kick your Casanova to the curb!*

\* \* \*

*Dear Allison, I was engaged to a man, who broke things off a week before my birthday. I still haven't been able to fully recover and it's been almost six months. I am grateful for the things I do have in my life, but do you see my situation changing at all for the better? Thank you. MK.*

*MK, consider yourself fortunate that your ex-fiancé figured out his feelings before you got married and not after you had a couple of kids. Six months isn't that long. It will take a while to heal from your break-up; although, just so you know, he will try and re-enter your life again so you'll be hearing from him. Be on guard when he calls and says, 'I'm just calling to see how you're doing.'*

*He'll be looking for an ego boost so be careful and protect your heart.*

*I believe that everyone we date teaches us something about ourselves—so, no regrets! There is someone out there for you who will want the same things that you do, so take your time finding Mr Right.*

## RELATIONSHIPS

* * *

I have been feeling that my relationship has run stale. My partner and I have a five-year-old son. I feel my partner took me for granted and held me back in life. He spent a lot of time with friends and spent all our savings. Since last April I have fallen for somebody else. Recently, I feel my new guy feels the same way about me, but he's three years younger, and not ready to settle down just yet. We have kissed and had moments but I don't want an affair and neither does he because he is friends with my partner. I'm okay with that for now, I just want to know what you see for me. Thanks, L.

*L, let's look at your situation carefully and piece by piece. You feel taken for granted by your partner, he spent all of your savings, and nowhere did you mention here still loving your partner romantically, not just as a friend! It seems you've already decided the fate of your current relationship, you just haven't made it official yet. So now your new 'flame' isn't looking to commit to you and he's friends with your current boyfriend? Well, that can't end well for any of you; my sense is that none of you will end up together! I know people get lonely and we all like to feel a spark of excitement to keep us young, but just be honest with your current partner about feeling like you should move on, because that's really what you've already done; moved on. Try and stay focused on your son. If you and your partner can part ways amicably, then your son will be much better off. And maybe down the road your current flirtation can turn into a healthy relationship, but let's be honest, could you ever trust one another? I see another child for you so be careful who you're with and make sure that you're ready.*

***

My husband and I have been married a year, we got engaged after six weeks believing we 'just knew'. It took him a while to act in a committed relationship and he's lied to me many times. I feel like I can't really trust him, and we are talking about buying a house and having children, and sometimes I think I'm making the biggest mistake. I love him so much—he's my best friend—but he has this female friend—I'm not controlling—it's just her, the way he is around her and talks to her and the things he says, like he 'can't not have her in his life because it would be like cutting off his arm'. I know he hasn't been unfaithful, but it hurts me so much. I feel like he doesn't want to choose me, but I want to trust him, I want to feel happy. Is our relationship going to last? Will things change? K.

*K, I know there are exceptions to the rule, but this is why the wise say to spend at least four seasons getting to know your mate! I'm just going to be straight up with you here—if Joe had a female friend and said that living without her would be like cutting off his arm, I'd help him with the saw ... just kidding! But seriously, anyone reading this knows the 'girlfriend' is clearly a threat to your relationship. You say he lies to you a lot but he's your best friend; those two statements don't go together. A true best friend would be upfront with you and this guy isn't upfront with you; he's playing some major head games with you! A house and kids, really?! You need to take a step back from this relationship and be totally honest with yourself, he's definitely got you* under his spell. My prediction is that if you stay, you won't be the only one pregnant with his baby. Take a deep breath and get your head in the game, girl! This public service announcement comes from one of your many 'sista-friends'.

* * *

I discovered my husband cheating again, two and a half years ago, and terminated my nearly 40-year marriage. Since then I've bought myself my own place, and have a steady professional job and loving and supportive family and friends. However, this has all shaken my confidence greatly and I still feel so sad, unsure and that life holds no joy. I have put on a lot of weight through comfort eating, which erodes my confidence even further, and I feel that no one would be interested in me because of the way I look. Can you see a good man in my future? Do I have something to look forward to in this, my later life?

Thank you, Allison.
Yours sincerely,
Lou

*Lou, I can understand you feeling depressed over your divorce; that would be devastating. When people have no confidence in themselves, they attract similar energy. So until you find a way to be content with yourself, you're not quite ready to meet a man. It sounds like you have a lot of wonderful people who love you and that would indicate that you have some fine qualities, so don't sell yourself short. If you can decide that you want to be the best that you can possibly be and push away the comfort food, you'll start to feel so much better. Remember that success is the best revenge so show your ex-husband that he made a big mistake, so strut your stuff! It's important to have a healthy state of mind when looking for a healthy new relationship so chalk up your ex-husband's actions to his bad judgement, the affairs were his fault, not yours. Become the person you want to be, and everything else in your life will fall into place. Good luck!*

\* \* \*

I also conduct a lot of relationship readings so I thought it would be fun to include some examples for you to get a glimpse of what they look like. I love getting feedback and seeing people find the affection they so desire.

Allison, I thought I would email to let you know how a piece of my reading with you has already manifested. I'm sure you read so many people, you probably don't remember mine, but you told me a couple of things in my phone reading with you several months ago.

You said I would meet a guy named Mick or Mickey, some derivation of the name Michael, and that he would be from Ireland. You said he'd make me laugh, and be very physically fit, and have a cute little accent. Later in our conversation, you suggested that I come out to where you live, in Arizona, to look for people to meet out there (I live in California). You specifically suggested I check out one particular resort.

Well, I've promptly booked a few trips to that same resort since talking to you—a couple of girls' weekends out there.

(Great resort, by the way! I love it!) One of the weekends I was there, I met a gorgeous guy. He lives there in Arizona. He gave me his business card and his first name was Michael.

The next day we were talking, and he said he hasn't lived in Arizona very long, only eight months. I asked where he lived before that and he said, "Ireland." You should have seen my jaw drop! He explained that he had lived in Ireland for a year. Later I asked him if he goes by Mike or Michael, and he said, "I'm fine being called either one. And actually, when I lived in Ireland, everyone called me Mick or Mickey."

Again, I just about fell over when he said that. Mick or Mickey from Ireland!

Another couple of things to mention about this guy: he is the epitome of 'physically fit'—*the most* cut, fit, muscular guy I've ever dated. He's in amazing shape and looks like a model. And he makes me laugh constantly. He's highly extroverted, the life of the party, funny and silly, so much fun.

So, Mick or Mickey, Ireland, makes me laugh, and physically fit: they all check off. The only thing is that he doesn't have a 'cute little accent'. However, he said that because he grew up in California, everyone in Arizona comments all the time on his Californian accent. I don't notice any accent, maybe because I live in California. But he definitely does talk like a surfer dude. Maybe that's what Arizonans mean when they point out our accents?

We hit it off great and spent the rest of that weekend together. I flew out again to see him last weekend, and we shared another great weekend together. I'm not sure if this would be a potential 'life partner' match; however, you didn't necessarily say he would or wouldn't be, anyway. In either case, he sure is a lot of fun to spend time with, and I'm very glad I met him. It was great timing, meeting him when I did: the fun, playful energy of our interaction has been a much-needed relief after some serious stuff I was just coming out of.

I wanted to let you know how dead-on you were, and how much fun it was to meet him, and be astounded at how accurately your reading manifested.

Thanks,
Michelle


## Happily ever after

### Kambria's story

I received my reading from Allison in February 2012, about a year after I'd ended an engagement. Doing a lot of work on myself and dating online for the first time, I was feeling confused and curious about my future.

Allison didn't beat around the bush when she explained that I'd been dating the wrong type of guys; they were very smart guys, but they were boring. She explained how it's all about them, how they're stuck on their path and not into having a relationship, but just want somebody there. Yup, that sounded familiar. She said I needed someone down to earth—someone with a firm handshake who cares about family.

She kept repeating the words 'back home', but the man she

saw for me was a smarter, more polished version of the guys I grew up with. She said we ran in the same circles, perhaps through a brother's friend. I wouldn't have to search because he'd be presented to me, and we had the same type of energy. She described how I'd feel so comfortable with him and he'd feel so comfortable with me; that we'd end up talking on the phone for hours. She assured me that ending my engagement was the right thing to do, and being single was the universe's way of saving me for the right person. I would end up married with kids, and being engaged within a year didn't feel far off, but I would have to be open to 'going back home'.

She told me this man was educated and had light hair and blue eyes, which was odd, given I'd mostly been drawn to darker features. She described him as charming and built, with a great smile. She said he was wonderful and waiting for me, that he would like and accept me as quirky and opinionated. He didn't feel like a doctor or lawyer, like my last two serious relationships, but instead he worked at his dad's company and had a business masters degree, but it wasn't a MBA. July was pivotal, she said several times; the strong relationship would come into the picture in July and I'd have to be open to 'going back home'.

During the following months, I felt incredibly hopeful about July! I had several dating experiences, but none of the men fit Allison's description and none had potential for me in the long run. As July came to a close, I was feeling less and less hopeful that Allison's reading was accurate. Where was this wonderful man that she described?!

Feeling disappointed, I went back to the online dating website to start the process up again. The search results presented an attractive guy and I felt compelled to 'wink' at him. He emailed back asking to meet me. As it turned out, we lived just four blocks apart and we scheduled a Monday happy-hour date, agreeing to meet on the street corner in between our homes.

Right away when he first hugged me and spoke to me, I felt so comfortable with him. Happy-hour led to dinner, and dinner led to a hand-holding walk around our neighborhood. The first kiss was overwhelmingly electric; on every level, our chemistry was intense, just as Allison had described.

When I got home that night, I realized that it was July 30$^{th}$. *Could it be him?!* He had a business masters, but not an MBA, and he was working as an intern in his first civilian job. He was blue-eyed with light hair, charming, built, had a great smile; and he was from 'back home' in Maryland (where I lived during high school). Just as Allison had described.

After spending the week thinking of each other, more than we had anyone else in a long time, we had our second date on Thursday. It felt as though we'd known each other our whole lives. During our conversation, comfortable and easy as ever, he told me how he had moved to San Francisco that year to be closer to his dad, recently diagnosed with cancer. In fact, he explained, he had learned about the internship opportunity from his father, who had just taken a medical leave of absence from the same company. I froze and couldn't speak for a moment when I realized that he had just told me that he worked for his father's company.

Again, just as Allison had described!

By that Friday, he told me he loved me, and he knew that I

*Relationships*

was the person he wanted to spend the rest of his life with, and by the next Wednesday, I had enough courage to say it back.

In the first week together, I learned that, as a pilot in the Marine Corps Reserve, he would be leaving for five months of military training in North Carolina, where I grew up. Was I open to continuing to date him while he was three thousand miles away? It was then that I realized he was absolutely the man that Allison had described. He was leaving to go 'back home' and, as she told me, I had to go!

Our five-month, long-distance relationship consisted of hours of phone conversations and me frequently taking trips 'back home' to North Carolina, just as Allison had predicted. We soon found out that we did, indeed, run in the same circles: his brother was close friends with a dear friend and classmate of mine. We were both in awe of how well Allison had described our connection.

After five months of dating, he moved in, and after nine months of dating, he proposed on the street corner where we first met. On June 7, 2013, shortly after ten months together, we were married at San Francisco, City Hall.

Allison just so happened to be in San Francisco the week we were married, which meant a great deal to both of us; she even tried to find us at City Hall during the ceremony! We will always think of her as a special and meaningful person in our lives.

Currently, we are searching for a home to grow our family. If you'd asked me a year ago, I'd never thought I'd be married to a Marine Corps major. However, just as Allison told me, I feel like I lucked out and the right person was worth waiting for; he was waiting right around the corner.

\* \* \*

Something that people don't know about me is that I'm a hopeless romantic! I know from talking to the dead that finding a great love in your life is important. Finding your match makes your life brighter and adds the *zing*! to your life experiences. I talk to so many living people who are looking for the great love of their life, and I'm thrilled when they find them. I swear that falling in love is the real fountain of youth! I always advise people to never settle for less in love because I see a lot of people panic and settle down with someone who's not right for them. I get people coming to me all the time who tell me how unhappy they are in their loveless marriage, and then the children they have are stuck in the middle. I believe everyone should search out happiness in life, and I know I'd rather have a happy life by myself than spend it with anything less than the love of my life.

I wish everyone had the sort of mate that a lifetime doesn't seem long enough to love them, you'd need an eternity! I'm always bringing couples through who choose to be together in the afterlife and relive all of their happiest days together. They still hold hands, they feed each other wedding cake on their wedding day, they play with their children, who are now grown in the living world, and they thank their lucky stars that they found one another.

For the record, when we went to City Hall in San Francisco, there were a lot of brides and grooms. However, when Joe and I were exiting, I saw Kambria and her husband-to-be going through security to enter the hall. I got to see the bride and groom and that was good enough for me; they looked enchanting … and they lived happily ever after.

So although I give advice to people who are looking for answers in their relationships, and I'm not always able to give them good news, it sure is nice to be able to see some happily-ever-afters come to fruition.

# Creating your version of heaven now

When you think of heaven, what would you like it to look like? Are you in a grassy field? Wading in the ocean with friends? Maybe at the kitchen table with your mother when you were small? Everyone has their own unique picture of what they want heaven to be, so let's design our heaven now, so that we aren't disappointed later, wishing that our picture had more color.

Take a minute to think about you in death—what would you want to come back and change? Wouldn't you say 'yes' to your kids more than 'no'? I mean, for the little things that make them happy, like a pizza for their classroom, an extra slice of birthday cake right before bed. Joe and I tried to give our kids magical childhoods; birthday parties with costumes made of balloons to act out a birthday play and pink champagne cake, building sandcastles on the beach on holidays, and seemingly endless slumber parties. We tell them that we love them constantly, and we make them laugh. Remember, you're creating your heaven and helping them to build theirs, too, so don't hold back, that's the only real regret that you'd have in death.

I always smile when I think of all of the doctors who cross over and are greeted by their deceased patients. These patients are there to thank the doctor for trying to save their life; they saw how much it weighed on the doctor when they couldn't. It's then that the doctor realizes that their efforts were appreciated. Most doctors give saving a life everything they've got, and they carry the burden of telling the family when they couldn't pull their loved one back from death. So you can imagine the warmth they feel when they see their deceased patients smile and extend a hand towards them, welcoming them to the light.

It's just as delightful when I think of animal rescuers or vets who cross over and are met by all of the animals they have helped, waiting to say thank you with a wag or a lick. People who spend their lives helping others often don't realize how many souls are supporting them from the Otherside. These souls who cheer us on throughout our lives are there waiting to receive us when we cross over.

The experiences that you have in life go with you, they become your reality when you die. People who take chances on love, and friendships, have plenty of souls waiting for them. The deceased greet them with a hug, kiss, handshake, whatever, and they are able to forever relive their glory days together.

For those who didn't connect with others in life, they're shown what they missed out on, and it's explained to them what they can do now to try and make amends with the living.

An easy starting point is to write down a list of things that you want to do before you die, and who you want to have these adventures with, in order to fulfill your 'heaven wish list'.

Speaking of heaven, I brought through a woman called Winnie for her daughter Nicolle, and the daughter had a question given by her son. He wanted to know, 'Is heaven real?' His grandmother Winnie responded with, 'There's a heaven on earth which is being with our loved ones. And there's a heaven for our soul also, with our loved ones, both living and dead. Heaven is all around you.'

I thought her answer was gorgeous! An older generation passing her wisdom down to her grandson, so that he won't take his family for granted in his young life. I also thought the grandson asked a great question, a question that builds on his spiritual connection to his grandmother. Even after death, our loved ones continue to guide us, teach us and help us to get the most out of our lives.

## Party of one?

Anyone who's been around somebody who's dying knows the conversations can be a little harder to navigate. Answers are harder to give, and there seems to be more questions than answers concerning death. A lot of people abandon ship when somebody's dying because they don't know what to say or they can't deal with the energy of the dying. I, on the other hand, think that we should do the opposite—we should celebrate the life of the dying while they're still here! Much like in the style of an

Irish wake, tell stories of your most favorite unforgettable times with them, raise a glass to them, everyone make their best dish and share it. Isn't it unfair that after someone dies we show them how much we care, but not while they're dying? The deceased do attend their funeral and memorials, but if you have the chance to show someone a good time before they die, do it! The dying are still among the living, show them they are, don't let the grim reaper have them just yet. They still belong with you.

When someone is dying, most people will scatter and go into hiding; it's a self-preservation tactic, it's as if the living think that 'death' is contagious. If family only shows up when a dying person is in a hospice, sometimes they feel like you're just waiting for them to die, and in reality you are. It's great to be there at the end, they do hear you and feel loved, just make sure you're there in the home stretch, too.

When my friend Domini was dying from cancer at the age of 31, I threw her a party, and I invited all the people that I could locate who knew her 'back in the day'. She was happy, she knew she mattered, she knew she would be remembered. Many terminal people would like a 'This is Your Life!' party while they can still enjoy everyone around them, and take part in the conversations reminiscing about the good times that decorated their life. I know that I'd rather enjoy the party while I'm alive, not after my funeral service.

## Angel on Earth

I've been fortunate in my life to attract some wonderful

people who I call friends. But we are all guilty of letting life get away from us and before we know it another year has ended. I want to share this story from my own life with you, so we can all learn to appreciate our friends now, while we're on the same side of the veil.

When our daughters were little, Fallon was seven years old and Sophia five years old, they made two very good friends who are sisters as well. I remember meeting their mother, JK, she had an infectious laugh, strawberry-blonde hair, and her two daughters were her whole life.

Over the years JK and I became friends as we watched our four girls make memories together at each others' birthday parties, school functions and pool parties. JK and I also made our own memories together, like when she came to our Halloween party dressed like a monk with bags of chips attached all over her frock. "Look, I'm a chipmunk!" she said. And there are everyday memories like the way she tossed her hair at the very moment that she wanted to emphasis something in the story she was telling us. JK could also eat endlessly but never gain an ounce! Her eyes had a light in them, the same light that a child has in their eyes when they're full of hopes and dreams. I loved her young energy, she was older than me but her energy wasn't older than mine—it was much, much younger!

So together we watched our daughters grow and before we knew it our youngest girls who use to cling to us were now taller than us. Joe and I had lived in Los Angeles for a couple of years and we both decided that we wanted to move back to Scottsdale to raise our kids. As soon as we'd settled in, we met up with JK and her girls again.

When JK pulled me aside and told me that she had a tumor in her brain, my heart dropped slamming to the pavement, and I was speechless. She told me she was about to be treated with a new form of chemotherapy, and she seemed hopeful. JK was one of the most upbeat, positive people that I've ever met, she was full of love and light. On January 27, 2014 I received a text from her, 'Feeling good ... let's not forget to get together ... it has been way too long. Enjoy your tour :~) JK'.

I was in Australia on tour for three weeks, then February flew by, March passed swiftly, in April I toured in the United States. On April 26$^{th}$ it was Fallon's birthday and my mind went to JK. I thought about Fallon's 'Sweet Sixteen' birthday party the year before, where JK and I sat for hours and talked. She was as bald as a billiard ball but very proud of her wig collection! It pained me to see my friend struggle, she possessed more life and love of life than most people you will ever meet. She told me that she wanted to be around for her girls more than anything in the world and—you know what?—she deserved to be at their graduations and weddings, see grandkids, Christmas, for all of that!

On April 27$^{th}$, we received a call to tell us that JK had passed away. The world had become less beautiful to me in that moment. To say that our family was devastated would be an understatement. Fallon and Sophia called JK's daughters in tears to express their support. Sophia cried on my shoulder and asked me the question that I've answered for countless strangers for years: "Why do good people have to die?" I really can't tell you have many times I've been asked that question, but to hear it from my own child stirred something deep inside of me, and it hurt, it ached.

I said: "Sophia, nobody would care as much if a bad person died. The good people make us want to do good things in their absence, they inspire us to be better, to do more, because we love them so much."

Then I held her, and in that moment she was four years old again and she needed her mom.

I was so worried about JK's girls; she was their rock and the voice that always told them, 'Everything is going to be okay.'

Children aren't prepared nor equipped to deal with losing a parent. I was 30 years old when I lost my dad, and I couldn't handle it—how were JK's teenagers going to move forward? Sure, I could take them to pick out their prom dresses, and attend their graduations and weddings, but it will never be the same to them. No one can ever fill their mom's shoes, not ever. I lost a friend, but they lost their one and only mother, and she was a spectacular woman!

Fallon took it hard, too. JK was like a second mother to my girls; she loved them unconditionally. Fallon sobbed as she told me how she went upstairs to play a song for JK on the record player that just days before she had been given for her birthday. She had put on an Elton John record that she had also received for her birthday earlier that day. "I picked a random song and it was 'A Friend's Funeral'," Fallon told me through her tears. I felt powerless to make it better for my girls. Being a medium, I knew that JK must feel powerless, too, watching the people who love her try and cope with her passing.

It was significant to me that JK's funeral would be at the St. Francis church. I hadn't been back there for a funeral since my dad's funeral ten years prior. Our girls were too young when my dad died to realize what they had lost. JK is the first memorable loss that our girls will endure in their lifetime, and it will stay with them forever.

We teach our children the beauty of life when they're small, as they grow and see things that aren't pretty, we have to be there to help them to navigate through disappointment and loss. Our daughters know what I do, now they're learning how my clients 'feel', and I want nothing more than to protect them from the pain. It's what every parent wants to do, shield their children from things that hurt. I know that JK must feel the same way; when people die they're forced to watch the living fumble through life while trying to find their lost loved ones again, to catch a glimpse of them, or hear their laughter one more time. JK will find a way to be heard by her girls, I have no doubt about that.

## WHERE HAVE YOU BEEN?

Three months after JK's passing, she paid a visit, but not to me. She came to my daughter in a dream (I'm not going to say which daughter because they are already hounded at school). My daughter came to me clearly shaken up and in tears, which broke my heart. I asked her what was wrong and she said, "I saw JK, Mom, and it hurts, because in my dream it felt like she had just died and I felt everyone's pain all at the same time."

I'm going to leave out some of the details because they're personal but what I thought was great was how my daughter described her: "JK was wearing a blue dress, her hair was long again, she didn't need a wig anymore. Mom, she looked really happy, she looked really good." My daughter told me that we were all sitting at the dinner table and JK was standing next to us. She said that in her dream she turned to me and said, "Mom, I see JK," and my response was, "I know, I see her, too." I'm not surprised that JK chose to come through to my daughter. JK knew she'd tell me about her dream and, besides, they had a close relationship. It was a weird feeling watching my daughter go through the emotional roller-coaster of having a 'visit'. I was proud of her, and thrilled for her, but I was also upset that she had to feel such enormous sadness. I passed on a gene that I can't take back, even if I wanted to. At least my daughter has me to talk to, to help her to interpret her information, and of course hold her for comfort. JK told me before she died that she'd be paying us a visit, and that I'd better let everyone know that she's fine. At the time she was being funny, but she was also serious. She wasn't ready to die. I promised her that I'd always be at her beck and call, anytime that she needed me. So here I am, passing on her message to you all—JK's happy, vibrant and just fine.

I think about my friend all of the time, I hug her girls, and I hope that she can feel them through my arms. One of the last times that I saw JK, she said that she was scared. I told her that, "It would be okay." I wish I could have meant it in the way that we both wanted, and not in the way that I said it, we both knew it was a long way from okay.

I've noticed that souls take on the form of metallic inflections in a kaleidescope that change form all around us as they morph into a beautiful vision, they have a sheen about them. They can shift from being 35 to five if they want to, visiting all of the best days that made up their lives. Many of my friends have become unique light since they died, something that we can appreciate but not quite grasp. JK is one of those visions now.

It hasn't escaped me that JK was a redhead mother-figure to our girls just like my friend Shari was to me when I was growing up. They're special women; actually, they are beyond any description or understanding of what 'special' really means, so we'll just call them *outstanding*. Sometimes I think about what JK would do in my shoes, and I instantly become a better person, she was a great measure of what the right thing to do is.

I sit beneath a sky, that most days are just fillers to people, not a reason to celebrate or embrace who we are, and I wonder what any of this means? There's world conflict that results in wars and people being hateful, wanting to do the wrong thing, out of selfishness or just because it makes them feel better to hurt others. But despite all the bad in the world, if you look closely, there's still something quite remarkable and alluring in the center of it all. Something so good and so perfect that it becomes our beacon home, it guides us to the best part of who we are, and that's more powerful than all of the bad combined. We're inspired by people who innately have to do the right thing, even though it wasn't required of them. All things good really do exist deep inside of us, goodness resides in our hearts and our souls, waiting for an opportunity to remind us all that we're more than good enough. We're here for a reason, to balance a heavy scale of right and wrong, even though it's not always easy. We do it for the people who lived before us, and, those who will come after us, who need someone to learn from. People need wisdom to help them in their journey as they search for spiritual evolution. We're all here to learn, some people are better students than others, but we all desire to be more than we started out as.

\* \* \*

Some years seem to pass free from any death and those are peaceful years. Other years we're not so lucky, and we watch people fall all around us. When I see pregnancies all around me, I actually worry because I know that when there's a baby boom, there's going to be passings, too. It's almost as if energetically the people who die are making room for new life.

Joe and I lost our dads at a young age but recently we've had to watch our friends go through a familiar pain, losing their own parents. As we stood next to our friends, dressed in black, as they focused all their energy on trying to keep it together, I felt useless. Yes, *me*—I couldn't fix this for them, I might be able to help them in time but, at the moment of the impact of death, nothing can be done from the outside.

Healing has to come from within. I can share my wisdom with the grieving but my advice can only ease their pain if they take it to heart and in the beginning it's sometimes too soon. When a heart is broken, we become deaf to the world around us as we no longer feel a part of it, because the world as we knew it has ceased to exist. We're forced to build a new world, one that will still hold our deceased loved ones, just not in the way it used to. Our new existence will be one that's chock full of weddings, babies being born, new friends and fresh experiences. Our deceased loved ones will be a part of all of those days, too, and they will cheer us on until we cross our own finish line.

As I always say, the irony of death is that the dead are more alive than we are!

INTO THE DARK